MEN
IN THE COMPANY
OF WOMEN:

A Provocative Anthology
of Praise & Persuasion

Edgar & Lenore's Publishing House
13547 Ventura Boulevard
Sherman Oaks CA 91423

ISBN: 0985471565
ISBN: 978-0985471569
LIBRARY OF CONGRESS CONTROL NUMBER:
2012955020

Printed in the United States of America

Editing & Cover design
by Apryl Skies & Alicia Winski
Artwork *Geisha & Michelle*
Carlos Scalise © 2012
Photo *Textures*
Apryl Skies © 2012

PREFACE

"The female of the species is more deadlier than the male..."
~ *from the album Spiders by Space*

While walking my dogs recently, I observed a thing of tragedy; a bright, green praying mantis obliterated by an impatient and perhaps unbeknownst motorist. I questioned whether this was the work of karma, fate, god, chance or something else entirely...

From the beginning of recorded time, the relationship between the male and female has been one of dynamic heartfire. Whether platonic or romantic, through shared DNA or otherwise, the male/female co-existence is without a doubt, a cosmic phenomenon of simplistic natural instinct and sublime perplexity; a true conundrum.

This collection of literature is so diverse in content a certain degree of laudatory contemplation and subjectivism is required for true appreciation. How would one toss the opinion of all men from across the globe; of all social divisions, cultures, religions, backgrounds and creeds into a cauldron, mix it up and come out with a hybrid of understanding that could remotely explain women in a true and effective light? That is a monumental task, indeed.

Some authors contained within are gentle giants getting to the heart of love. Others get right to the gut of loss scooping out life experience as it comes. Through their musings, they swallow joy and compassion like fine wine, wallow in loss and regret or use humor, dark or otherwise as a tool of healing and survival.

With the general public in mind, this is not a book specifically for the bibliophile seeking a purely Shakespearean, romantic view through the shades of some polarized rosy lens, but it does encompass that. Nor is this a book mainly for the reader in search of a fly's perspective from the wall of the red light district, however, that may also be represented: Nor is this a book for those with a misogynistic, plastic view of the female, however, depending on your perspective, this may be on the menu as well.

Some difficult subjects may be contained within: drug use, suicide and domestic abuse, so the easily offended, delicate-minded would be strongly advised to look elsewhere.

This is a book for the reader seeking truth, wishing to unlock what men honestly think when they look at women, into their eyes, soul, heart and life; what they feel, what they know and have experienced. It represents what they not only despise, resent, regret but, ultimately love and admire In the Company of Women.

Glamorous or not, beautiful or awkward, vicious or kind, rejected or embraced, this collection of poetry, fiction, and non-fiction is no less than gentle, brave and a true contemporary gem.

Apryl Skies

FOREWORD

"This is a man's world, this is a man's world, but it wouldn't be nothing, nothing without a woman or a girl"
                                        ~from *This Is A Man's World* by James Brown

My heart has been stolen and I am a woman in love. I am a bigamous lover, however. For I, like millions of women who have been broken, vowing never again to walk into the tender trap only a man can set, have fallen in love yet again, and this time, with over 100 men from around the globe; *MEN IN THE COMPANY OF WOMEN*

I have handed my heart, sliver by sliver, to remarkable men gifted with tender sensibilities in absolute confidence that they will be held gently in deft hands united in a very special brotherhood.

Stumbling into adulthood, I settled, as many women do, into comfortable pre-conceived notions of what I perceived male perception to be and my assumptions have radically reversed during this literary evolution. Every word read brought honest and often brutal revelations of masculine intimacies bore for viewing. In *'LOSING MY BEST FRIEND TO HEROIN''* by Timothy Gager, the perceptions I've always held about men in general as being emotionally impregnable were dissipated by stark words of regretful and reluctant acceptance of a friend's determination to self-destruct. It was with surprise that I found myself reading so many encounters of addiction shared by this group of writers and their various reactions to it. Two prime examples are *'INSULATION'*, by Jerry Garcia, a beautifully sardonic view of a woman's addiction as seen through the eyes of the writer and *'STIGMATA'*, a gut-wrenching tale of a woman's self-mutilation and eventual death through overdose told by Arne Torneck.

Weaved into, and softening these grievous truths, are powerfully moving sentiments of love in many forms, be it the romantic love for a woman, the power of a son's love for his mother, or the far too often repressed love of a man for his daughter. Dom Gabrielli's voice, in *'MY ANGEL'*, is an almost guttural and moving cry of a father determined to instruct a beloved daughter in the realities of life and love while admonishing her to stand strong; to maintain the knowledge of who she is and where she comes from; harsh lessons penned with a surprisingly delicate hand. In *'WARM SALT'* by Kevin Craig, a helpless husband chastises a deceased wife for leaving behind the results of her fatal addictions; a young daughter to be raised without the love and guidance of a motherly hand.

The misconception of stalwart men remaining granite in the face of gut-wrenching grief and helplessness is also blown out of the water in horror film master (American Horrors) Hart D. Fisher's, 'GOD DUG A SHALLOW GRAVE IN MY HEART', an enormously moving ode of loss and longing for a love murdered in her prime and in his 'RIO' a piteous saga of emotional and physical abuse by a woman against her lover.

Upon these pages lie proof that tender musings and longings for love are not confined to the Ovary Calvary alone. In fact, with 'THE THINGS I WOULD TELL YOU...IF WE EVER MET' by Duane Kirby Jensen delivers a lush Monet dream flowing like a quiet river, while lovely and tender musings are quietly whispered to us in the contemplations of Taylor D. Mackintosh through 'THOUGHTS OF YOU'. The wonderment of woman is shared with us via the epitome of charm and chivalry in 'DIALOGUE', by Sumio Matsuda, a beautifully written and moving poem, found and so graciously submitted to us posthumously by his son Robert Matsuda.

One of the most affective writings within this collection is MOTH LIGHT for Grace Paynter' by Pushcart Award nominee, William Crawford, author of 'ACTUAL TIGERS'. This lovely ethereal poem, is a simple, gentle observation of a beloved face stamped with time told in a quiet and admiring voice.

All in all, the magnitude of what these men, in their musings, writings, anecdotes, and, yes, their confessions, have shared in this collection of work is astounding. Within these pages is a lesson; that if men and women are ever to reach a true understanding so often deplorably unattainable, and one that should have been obvious to the feminine gender all along: When it comes to matters of the heart, there is really very little difference between the sexes; we all bleed red.

This is proven by the gentlemen gracing this anthology and sharing a wealth of knowledge in raw and touching stories humbly presented in the hope that their readers might walk away with a greater appreciation of what they may very possibly have spent their prior years taking for granted; the men I love, these remarkable, Men In The Company of Women.

Alicia Winski

WOMAN & MUSE

THERE is nothing, absolutely nothing,
No flower, no tree, no snow-capped mountain,
No babbling brook, no river or stream,
No diamond, no pearl, no shiny sports car,
No gleaming mother-lode of gold,
No animal, no mineral, no exotic tropical isle
No sunrise or moon shimmer
No sacred sonnet or symphony
As beautiful, in this wandering world,
As a beautiful woman.
The long silk hair, the skin like satin,
The smooth, curvy legs, the rotating buttocks,
Those round and rosy breasts…
Here, they grow like weeds:
At every street corner, at every supermarket queue,
At every reception booth, at every turnstile and stand,
At every and all outstanding male fantasies,
There they are, staring down
From every theatre screen, every magazine counter,
Every topic and newspaper ad.

There they are
And here we continue to grovel
Like wide-eyed urchins
Staring at a storefront window of savory delights
At the unlikely prospect
That one of these celestial visions might
Like Newton's apple,
Fall freely and without hesitation
To the tired and blistered feet
Of this mere mortally-grounded man.

JR Phillips

IN ADORATION OF WOMEN

Every woman deserves a poem
a line of sweet and gentle verse
a recitation cuddlesome
saying she is your universe.
Every woman needs a flower
laid on her breast each sunny morn
a gift of passion in her bower
where love is endlessly reborn.
Every woman requires a kiss
bestowed upon the break of dawn
a lush and blushing touch of bliss
as tender lips worship and fawn.

Around the alter of her flesh
charmed angels dance for this goddess.

Michael H. Hanson

DIALOGUE

Like the music of
some rare stone, her words
expressed an inner

shape that she could not
conceal, her art was
so compact of innocence.

And though, complete
within herself, she talked
to me of surfaces,

what I heard
was only that shape;
and her stance,

her very occupation
of space, was really
what she said.

Sumio Matsuda

18

FROM YOUR SYLLABLES (7/30)

for my mother

your mother holds your name in her teeth
so that it stays warm on her tongue
safe behind her grinning barricades
she holds your name there
savoring just the thought of you
through every off key circumstance
and every abraded encounter
her vocabulary will negotiate a song
a gospel foxtrot lullaby
from your syllables
her exhalations will seed your wisdom
and even the most transient
of absent-minded hums
will declare war on your lazy boredom
fireworking your dismay

she will hold your name
where she holds all of her truths
in the place from where
spring the metaphors of her eternity
she will hold it like a precious private dialect
as a symbol of her generosity
of all the things she has given this world
in the shape of you

your mother will hold your name
as if it is the only thing she would ever want to taste
as if there were no cemetery walls on which to scrawl it

she will hold your name and cry
she will hold your name
and swallow a cocktail of the unrelenting
the unarticulated need of you
the unexplainable joy of you

she will hold your name in her teeth
while all that is important repeats
and when the mystery rises into her eyes

she will turn to you and finally speak
and that is when you will know what it is

David McIntire

HARDLY A BUTTERFLY
(for K.)

the dark times
bring the most songs

too soft
these voices
for this
solid air

breath's promise
arrives dead
hangs insincere smile

cynical finger
pokes at nothing

the lightning exceeds
its own grasp

you never asked
to be its rod

judging shape
of subject
judging shade
inside object

here's a wish,

end all stories
like dreams

i.e. no more conclusions

the faceless keep
their empty distance

ignorant to mother's
trembling hand

reaching out from the stable
forming natural bridge,

she says…

William Crawford

OVER THE VILLAGE
Based on the painting by Marc Chagall, 1924

As long as we are light with light,
our feet will never touch the ground again ---

        floating over night-time houses
into the moon, we are locked in sleeper's embrace.

Do not say, there are things more important that this ---

        our slippers are stardust,
our testimony ---
we are so in love, we do not notice other people
opening their dark windows, leaning into our swirling love,
wishing they were this dedicated,

        we notice none of this ----
we skim the curve of air,   below,
other lovers are lifting as violin notes.

Martin Willitts Jr.

THE CURBED RIM OF LOVE

The ocean drank my wrist
The summer took my spine

On odd days
I look for you

On even days
I don't have to

The oar hit the
Waters of the bayou

Like my head once did
The termites of your ventricles

Long and hard
And without thought

In the possibility
That like you I could
Be perfect

But like love
I am neither
Good nor bad
Ether nor orchid

Radomir Vojtech Luza

MOON POEM #3
To Bronwen

Moon, steal
Steal through the shadows
Slink through the clouds
Steal away all light, colour
Make all ghostly white
Translucent as the shell-whiteness

Of her skin.

Moon, steal
Steal away the light from the corners
Make all black, black
Drowned in the purple
Shadows, indian night
Sharpen the edge of the darkness
So that recalls her dress, black sheath
In which dwells the white dagger
That cut my heart

Moon, steal
Take away from me these memories – oh!
Her hands folded in her lap
White tuberoses
And bloody lips
Soft as the peeled skin of mushrooms
Picked in the dew before dawn
Moon, thieve from me the knowledge
Of how she says my name.

Moon, moon, we are all thieves
Rogues staggering, drunken
Through the deserted streets
Of a fat town

And her eyes, like hazelnuts
A vagabond's eyes
Inviting me to play – Ah!
Moon, steal
Give my tongue the wings

That see you span the world in a night
Moon, give me the words
To steal her heart away.

Thomas Kent

THE BREEZE

If you look at them just right
You can see exactly what's hiding behind her eyes

It's the twilight hiding beyond the moon reflecting sunlight
It's brighter than the smile she lets loose every once in a while

And every once in a while I catch her do it
And every so often I let her catch me catch her doing it

But truthfully, all I'm catching is my breath
Or just trying to do my best
Because the way this girl looks, looks good
To every man within a glance

The way this vision sings rings in everyman's head
Like the last song he heard on the radio instead

And the way this girl moves
Dances as delicate as danger does

While her hair wisps behind her
Bouncing in the wind

All as she floats by

Jason Brain

HOW SHALL I IMAGINE YOU?

How shall I imagine you,
        tiny word under my heart?
With pen or thought — a phantom start
        to capture who you are?

How shall I envision you,
        soft feather of my wing?
With brush or mind, begin to sing
        of your plain intricacy?

How shall I respire you,
        momentous breath of air?
With lung or hope — but both unfair
        your weight to justly say?
And if I weigh
        you with a word
        when you are absent,
will you not have heard
        my admiring footsteps, present
                in your soul?
And if I drink you with a memory,
        will you not remember me,
the water sweetly soothing
        till you're full?

I imagine you a thought —
        a phantom feather — not
subdued by my expression,
for that would be oppression; let it show
        that you were free, but now forego
        your right to light on wings your own,
and, nestled in mine, you make your home.

You were the red feather of my plumes,
        unfit for dark gray ranks,
but you were filled for me with fumes
        of life, strong veins of which I drank.
And now, instead,
        my beloved bled,

28

every feather of mine red,
you dyed me,
    and I died to thee.

After you were taken in,
    my wings were colored life, and flight
grew softly once again.

Evan Dunn

ALLEREDNIC

I walked in darkness and an angel
found me or I found her
I never could be sure
and though she'd lost her wings and halo
she took me close enough to heaven
while she kept my feet on the ground
it is the story of my three loves
but heaven was never quite what I expected
it has its own demands and strictures
even when it stays close to Earth
I walked out of one, not sure I was ready
I lost one, sure I was unready
and so far have worked well enough
to remain in the third
thank you, angels, for all the ways you cared
for loving me when you did, and loving me as you do
I'm pretty sure no heaven awaits me when I die
but how could I need it, having shared yours?

Wyatt Underwood

CONFESSION OF A LOVE JUNKY

My thoughts race to heaven's expanse,
hoping to find you waiting to embrace them.
Knowing you will find answers to share,
guiding my appeal for comfort in clouds
surrounding you.

I am standing beside you
on the axis of secret vistas.
While you read my message,
as part of the wind touching our souls.
Two kindred spirits, joined by words of
poetic expression, hope, love, and desire.

I am present in each thought you share,
as part of me exists in every grain
of sand moved by the wind of you.
Wondering which part you would keep
closest to the heart of your being?
I pray it is my lips, softly saying your name.

I am the thorn and crucified palm.
You are both pleasure and pain.
For the sake of Love's lessons you are
an addiction. You are narcotic in my veins.
Blood flows like ink on the page of true
confessions. I need you to complete me.
You are the rush and exhaustion of my soul.

RE Smith

MOTION

her voice was like falling bricks
and her smile was shattered mirrors
and i would joyfully surrender myself
to her rhythms
and her compulsions

we found a way to dance together
that embarrassed neither of us...too much
and we found a way to teach each other
i couldn't tell you what she learned from me but...

i learned not to try to catch the bricks
that it was much more beautiful to see them hit the ground
i learned how to comb my hair in her smile

that it was all in motion anyway

David McIntire

AN UNEXPLAINED GAP IN TIME

She slips, she moves indifferently
Through courtiers of her ancient heart
With the capacity to undress the night
Into the barest hours
Where I watch her all the time
Making circles unattach
Running rings around me
The shape I cannot catch
Is faster than the eye can see
Bur slower than my heart
Like an unexplained gap in time
She keeps me in the dark
Where I must be part of her
Like the shadow on her back
The pulse within her wrist
And the speed it does not lack
Beats out all the tiny sorrows
In her dungeon where she keeps
The time between her desperate hours
I know I must dig deep
To release each anxiety
That labours in her day
The cages of her fears
Which obstruct the only way
That we can be together
And watch our lives unfurl
In an unexplained gap in time
I lock myself into her world

Spencer Slater

WAKING

He woke and wrote what he could remember.
He never dreamed when he slept here.
Now he wanted to dream more.
He felt aggrieved somehow and tore
the paper from the typewriter
without looking at the black marks.
Her eyes were sky blue. He kissed her ears
everywhere, one then the other.
There were words for sounds he never
heard himself play before.
It was some time since he played clarinet.
How could he pick it up and play like that
now composing on the pulse of an hour?
Much simpler to keep dreaming.

Floyce Alexander

MY ANGEL

love inflicts wounds which do not heal

and you cry nightly
playing digital dominoes with future loves
dreaming of growing up to be a fighter and a lover
like your ma and your pa
when they took on the world

you know too much of who you are
and why you are

unborn years weigh upon your innocence

Aphrodite herself gestures to the wall
saying listen to the sea

the aromas of the outside
swell beyond

take the boat out to sea
the drunken boat
the boat of dreams
the boat of nights
of tides and stars
and shooting lights

never be afraid
nor of the dark nor the light

you will ever be my girl

i told you before
love should never be an obsession
it cannot be sought
it cannot be captured
because it does not live within beauty
never within a face within a body
nor can love be given like an infliction
it cannot be implemented like a strategy

it lives when the moment allows freedom

the reigns to pull in the tides

between the horizon and dawn
your tears will flow

yes i am talking to you
you who were born to me
born of lovers
born of fighters

yes i fought for you
for your breathing lung
for your pale mediterranean skin
for your large brown eyes
for your fierce temper

i fought for you my angel

what do these schoolmasters know of love
with all their punishments up their sleeve
with all their drowning gulps of envy

i was not taught to write at school
i was taught how not to write
how not to think
i was told to leave love at the gates of the castle

one day they said write a poem
they said write a poem in thirty minutes
i did not know what a poem was
but my hand would not stop
blackened tears of another sun
and the schoolmaster looked at me
did you write this
and as i nodded he mused as he had never mused
are you sure you wrote this he replied
and i bowed my head in shame
and he said it is remarkable
i did not think you capable of writing this
and i walked away wondering who had written that poem

was it really me or the stars or the light rains of another moon

you spoke once of the sun and its pink blanket

you were five
you told me the sun must go to sleep too
to dream of rainbows and swift swallows

the world is at my bedside you know
there is a pulse
i cannot explain it further

our eyes have poems in them girl
they write songs to the storm clouds
they speak of summersaults of freedom

how much silence
how many bowed heads
how many moments trampled upon
and left to die
how much waste
how much jealousy in their scorn

silence is the only strategy
silence and a sea of words
and a look in the deep black of our eyes

i have wandered it is true
i have wandered far and wide
i cannot tell you everything
i must let you grow
i must let your poems grow with you
piece by piece you will make your own puzzle
day by day you will draw your own portraits

do not give yourself away
to one who cannot read the poems in your eyes

i never lost this invisible key
even when i was yet to find it

i was only lost in my own silence

there are many signs to gather
there are many paths to roam
until you roam no more

one day i will hand this key to you
it will be yours to share
it will rest in your beloved hand for a moment
just as my dead father's ring
rests upon my writing finger

forever

Dom Gabrielli

BLUE EYES

Such - beautiful - blue-eyed-sadness
wrapped in a white dress that covers
a body - yearning for touch - for tender,
yet manly touch. Your lips part - and wait,
and wait, and wait - for warm lips to respond
to your longing. A first kiss that will unlock
your becoming - and usher in the death
of innocence.

Your eyes are the eyes of Ophelia,
before she slipped - beneath,
the purity of a cool brook.
I see you - a creature of flesh - and wonder,
How did you escape - those ink-stained-pages
of Bronte?

From - I Cannot Remember Their Names: Selected Poems,
Three Frogs Swimming Publications
Duane Kirby Jensen

URANUS V

… my dear one, thee, my daughter, who
Art ignorant of what thou art.
                    (Shakespeare, *The Tempest*)

Your terrain is a Shakespearean row,
cratered with Alonso, Prospero, Trinculo,
squabbling three billion kilometres from Milan,

all now castaways in the wrong plays,
coronae of Arden, Elsinore, Inverness,
regiones of Mantua, Sicilia, Ephesus,
a Birnam Wood-less Dunsinane,

a geological intertext of catastrophes,
cryovolanic eruptions, tectonic uprisings,
canyons, chevrons, *sulci*, Verona *rupes*,
a cataclysmic collage of script-shatterings
pasted back together by gravities,

a motley world of places you wouldn't know,
of other people, father, lover, king, fool:
here you're never your own true self –
that Mirandian self who's much nearer home.

Jonathan Taylor

MAMAN'S KISS

Today, we take the shorter way
And I see a scudding row
Of low, far off trees
Tonight we'll dine on time

Tomorrow, we may take the royal way
More beautiful than light
But more dear, for
Then our meal will be late

And the cost? A kiss. Not much
But refused, I'll sob as
The moon touches
The purple, fecund fields

The memory of her azure aurora
Calls across the time, lost
But I remember as
My childhood falls away

Princesses and barons lie ahead
I'll know their nights
Oh – too well
Still, it's her kiss I'll recall.

Dan Capriotti

DRINKING IN THE STAR-HUNGRY DARK

My lover and I sit with Black Russians,
slumped against two tree stumps
like old laundry along the banks of Kern River.
This evening, we braved its rapids
on our cooler roped to two chairs,
our peanut-shell foreheads piercing
the muddy milk-blue surface film,
bobbing between the twin worlds of the fish
and their educated cousin, the snake.

My lover and I sit with black
quilts covering our shivering bodies.
The fire between us rises skyward,
impotent to penetrate the moon,
who must surely see us shivering here,
as she laughs her slicing lightning,
and all life folds into her toothless smile,
leaving only a dark purple plum
budding from Orion's astral wound.

I slice into a plum tree's arm,
revealing the raw, green exchange
of oxygen between us,
as my own leaf-veined lungs expand
and contract with the Universe
collapsing into the star-hungry night. I bite into
a plum, and I know this sweet Earth is just
fattening my body up for the wind to dissolve
like laundry on a line flung heavenward.

Matthew Nadelson

ORIGINS

Who is the master mistress of this site,
ancient cave above amniotic water,
sacred to Eileithuia, goddess of child birth?
To the foot of her stalagmite I crawled
like a new born, found a coin in Asia Minor forged
in the same century as he who guided me
torch in hand to her fenced off shrine
beneath the ground. Perhaps it was his coin,
in front, face of Alexander,
on the reverse, Perseus, mere drachma
belying the mighty. Had Pausanias
dropped it here, one of his offerings
to the Cretan women walking their round,
groaning Olen's song to her? Homer too
pays tribute to Eleutho but by way
of his disguised hero claiming to have seen
himself here, as if every mother's son.

But history and lore elide a greater story.
How many wailed here in the dark
torch light? How many died?
How many returned battered but blessed
back into the sun? Every mother's child,
we are born of heroes back from the brink.
No goddess, warrior or emperor can steal
their courage though in darkness unsung
they have labored for whatever we are worth.

Thousands of years later, I recall the birth
of my son, how the doctors toured
the insides of my wife as I watched
from above, reduced to stroking her head,
unable to ease her fear for the child -
though I feared for her more. He was

43

so big they had to lift him out, purpled
and sheathed in vernix from the cave
where he formed. Into her weary arms
she took him after she awoke from darkness -
and as he looked up into her eyes, only then
did she smile, both of them, free.

Anthony Di Mateo

ARTEMIS

How could he help but stare,
Acteon, skilled huntsman,
Marksman with arrow, keen-eyed,
Quick-footed, forager of forest
And glen?

And Artemis alone in the water,
The chaste goddess, naked from the knees,
Dazzling the eyes of the stunned huntsman,
Stunned and startled by the visage
Before him.

Rash in judgment, void of passion,
Impervious to the lure of libidos,
She with her sorcerer's skill and willful vexations,
Made stag of man, hound's meat, the hunter
Now the hunted.

And the carnage she craved,
The blood-splattered earth, the testicles torn
And the manhood mangled,
Somehow seems oddly unsuited for one so protective
Of the wild.

Destined to deny that which the gods
Had intended,
Protector of the woods, fertility's goddess,
She chose a chasten rage, guardian
To the Feminist manifesto.

JR Phillips

RENAISSANCE NOW PROM NIGHT

I thank thee for the grace of thine society. Your eyes however were the more voluminous and storied than a bard has words. Those gestures made on behalf of a dwarf and others in defiance of convention and judgment by which you endeared thineself so as to be the essence of a Renaissance poet's inspiration. Not of this time but of one whose like has not been beheld since Guenevere passed into legend.

I thought I had strayed into a world grace once more with princesses worthy of the name. Proved you tender hearted as you are beautiful. Though the music was far less than gentile it mattered not for thou art the only music known this world, you were princess as ever envisioned. I couldn't hear the harpsong for that which was sonorous in your laughter. Your green dress served to bring out your beaming vivacity all the more strikingly. The effect was positively bewitching though you had more so of the angel.

My Lady of the Dal-Cais, if but for the duration of an evening beneath the stars. What need one of the stars anyway when they have the honour of dancing with you. Though bardic poetry is now bygone from mind but more so the heart as the warrior of armour . I think it never wrong to acknowledge beauty.

I hope that the years have brought more smiles to thine beauteous countenance than tears and continue to do so. From the vibrant sway of your glorious red hair aflow in impossibly fiery resplendence, to your constelled freckles that adorned thine smiling face. You are as ever loveliness itself. What more can be written about a lady who is a poem. I will always remember you as my lady of the dance.

Autumnal and twilight red beauty ever to match the brightness of your smile and the grace of your person. Know that you were and will always be the matchless one. I trust your days will treat you accordingly and the warmth that your friends regard you will be rewarded in kind. Princess then and now.

Had you debuted in the court of Prince Lywellyn of Wales: the harpsong would have ceased for the bards would have been struck dumb. The last warrior chieftain of the free Cymru would have doffed his helm and said respectfully: "My Lady welcome home. We missed you." gesturing to a throne.

I could compose more bardic tribute but how could I even write in tribute to you if you are a poem itself. There is respite and quiet to devote to writing. The reason I wrote is that I found your vivacity and laughter not just infectious but truly heart melting. I came across the portrait you were so gracious to stand with . Not even Raphael could do you justice. The memories sparked the poetic muse and I felt as if I should write. It is always the poets joy to receive a compliment to the lady of his inspiration. It made my heart dance again. You truly lit up the room so as to evoke the honeyed words: "Oh she doth teach the torches to burn bright".

It has often been said that William Shakespeare's plays can be staged or enacted in every era as human aspirations are timeless. Then so I have writ in tribute to one who has exemplified the attributes of leading lady and being Renaissance woman have cast her in environs more befitting one who seems stepped from canvas and illumined manuscript.

As one does not have to don the trappings of the medieval to be knight a coronet of gold no makes a queen than shorn mane unmakes a lion.

Greg Patrick

MISMATCHED COUPLETS FOR THE GODDESS, WHO WILL NOT TARRY

Char, grit, libation, wine, incense,
spry-footed *ghazal*, in the classical Arabic sense,

there is a whiff about you, something of the impatient.
I sometimes dream myself the nascent

vision clenched behind closed eyes in alabaster.
That's how you come to me: faster

than Macedonian conquest.
Each child shall memorize Homer at your behest,

I will it, for you,
and this: that the world should be as a drop of dew

upon the hill of some high city, shining
bronze in the equatorial light, with the garish paint still lining

the statues; and we will look out through the water
where a gold-haired tradesman's daughter

draws from a clay jar her favorite stylus,
pressing the fingers of a hexameter, lines that beguile us

into the worst of offenses, the hubris of certainty
(praise, then, to Doubt, at the close of the curtain). Be

what you will: what you have granted will suffice.
Your lines slice

open the heart, then mend it as one reclaims a time-ravaged fresco.
Extend your hand to me—let's go

dancing, drunk in the woods, as though Pentheus
had loosed his grip, no longer bitter, no longer envious—

and limbs entwined in metamorphosis, I'll tell you with a laugh
how your initials make a cryptograph.

Scott Miller

MY VENUS, FOR YOU I CAST A SPELL

I shall to my hand a candle fetch
Candle small of plainness, of pure white
I as a lover, a fool, a wretch
Shall place it, and with match will light
And bring forth an Aisling[1] of you
Coming to me as I desire
I shall watch it, as candles do
Burn by wick to base with the fire
Having nothing of yours as mine
I shall your image, and mine too
Remembering desires thine
Horses image so loved by you
I shall watch the candle burn to base
Accept the love I get with grace

Tomás Ó Cárthaigh

---

[1] Aisling – gaelic for vision, imagining

Poem based on a folk spell for a man to bring a woman he desires to him, get a white candle, an object of image of them both, and an object or image of something the one desired liked. Candle was to be burned, watched by the desirer, who brings to mind an image of the desiree coming to him, watching the candle burn to base. All the remains and the images, to be kept together, the love, if any to be accepted with grace.

GYPSIES

Your hand on my leg feels like a sack of grain.

I'm full of skillet fixins,
lukewarm coffee
and the orange juice
I should have avoided.
It always makes me anxious.

Their voices quivered over breakfast
and sang over dinner last night.

A Shakespearean profusion
of Island tales
and dining room gossip. Touching.

But I do not want
to be touched
without greed,
without desire.
Your hand on my leg feels like
a sleeping child.
Weighty and adhesive.

It's for you.
It's something you need.
So I oblige it.

I could've broken my wrist
jumping over the balcony like that,
in slow motion.

In that moment, I too was old and forgetful.
I'm sweating a little in my jeans underneath the place
your hand is resting on my leg.

If only you could need me a little less than I fear you do.
If only we could be like two gypsies wanting only a companion
for a journey without an end.

Kenyon Adams

WALKING DOWN RIVER BEND

A walk through misty morning's kiss
Steps crunch graveled street car tracks
Under ancient oaks in moss
Tossing wordless pledges back
Kept where humid truth is rendered
Silence swept in blue surrender
This full heart and soul for you
Art like trinkets shined with dew
Open ended wet commitments
Splenda'd coffee sentiments
Fairy tales on joined hands swinging
As the singing gravel wails

Tell me Love what moves this moment
Tell me how to help you grow
Sacred Morning holds us closer
Bound where secret breezes flow

Once an inch below your ear
My lips lingered then to throat
Fingertips to cheek and stroke
Like sparrow's flutter fate is cleared
A new life written by the minute
Lost in your eyes years could fall
Calling God's to keep me lucid
Like your knight post'd strong and tall
I'd spend it all for what we did

You said you heard I conquered Europe
"I loved them more than they loved me;
They wanted Dixie; I am funky
So three clinics? Wow I'm thrilled;
I'm sorry. Three? How many years?"

And as the mist to rain soft spilled
We found the old Camellia Grill
"Batiste brother start a bill"
May be awhile before it clears

Dwayne St.Romain

THE RIVER

Fingers reached out
Joined
Made a hand
That became
An arm
A shoulder
The tall torso
Of a country girl

Drinking
The incessant
Liquids of the fields
You grew

Muttering
Endless truths
To yourself
Amidst the
Grey stones

I watched
Trees
Sweep past
Curtsying

Horses
Curl past your banks
Like a roundabout

The fat
Slick
Bodies of rats
Plock into your holes

Fowl gliding
Effortlessly
Pushed by
Invisible hands
Yet secret
Underneath

Red webs churning

Eels
Scarves of steel
Nuzzle into the ooze

I shared at night
Your vanishment
Black vein
In dark grey fields
Only the glint
Of white satin
Betraying your
Invisible presence

I helped sardines
Eager for the antipodes
Escape your eager grasp

I helped frantic salmon
Leap your
Laughing rapids

Your still surface
Your listlesss depths
Sheets wrinkle
Then pull smooth

From far up
Where you are
A sliver of silver
Between the stones

To the end
When you spread
Your turgid self
Between the arms
Of the estuary

I knew you.

Thomas Kent

BYBLIS UNBROTHERED

When in winter we fell ill, our body-
heat was all we had to keep warm.
We would take baths together, gathering

lavender and jasmine from the garden
to warm with water in cast iron pots,
and pour the boiling petals in the tub.

Oh, spilling deliverance of water
over breasts ripe as Early Girl
tomatoes sealed in their own sweat.

I wonder what she must have felt
when I caressed them.
Such suction of an open nerve

rooted deep in the rotten soils
of our neurosis, must have surfaced
an old, deep pattern of fraternal love.

She says we would have been a good
mother/son or father/daughter.

She was my sister, not by blood but water.

Matthew Nadelson

IMPRESSIONS FROM A CERTAIN PAINTING BY SEURAT

Let me point out things I know she must do,
this kept woman, if indeed she's kept, very proper,
almost properly attired, she must turn to her right,
nod and smile on this informal occasion, she did not don
facund gloves or bring frilly fan, her familiar man surveys
the grand isle of Arcadian contentment before them.

The steel monkey leashed around the waist,
the stolen monkey definitely kept as pet, *singesse*
as named, "Je ne sais pas á siffler,"
leashed so as to not choke to death,
nor bite, nor slip easily away,
leashed in the manner found
on the family crests of knaves,
she must stand rigid in the shade
holding monkey chains loosely,
not breathe in too deep lest she sneeze,
no reticule, no nettled tissue to stem
light ridicule, stem eyes rolling away
from sleeveless bodice, she is no doll,
no droll child, and he must bow
and offer embroidered handkerchief
with hand not holding cigar.

Fewer petticoats withstand summer heat,
Paraguayan parasol blocks out summer sun,
she might twirl such about like Eliza Lynch,
obsequious milliners steal all summer fun,
Sondheim wrote there never was a hat
where there never was a song about a bonnet
on a bonne lass.

Her chemise hides her stature,
whether rose stained or starchy white,
Pissaro yellow degraded to ochre
standing stiffly staring in the park.

Angel Uriel Perales

OLD WOMAN IN PARIS

she said
Pablo told her
to keep doing
what she loved

not
to care
about others
even
if she grew
desperate
broke
sure she'd
wasted
her life
& I said
nothing

stuck wishing
I'd lived
then & had some

of that wine
with them

Mark Wisniewski

THOUGHTS OF YOU

I stretched my legs
and sighed aloud asking myself

where did we begin?

I tried to find that first moment;
and I quickly realized

it's always now

I always care, I always miss you
I think of life without you and wonder

When did we begin?

Where did we start?

… the same place we never ended,
the same time we never finished …

Taylor D. Mackintosh

The Ends of the Earth
Based on the painting Le Bout du monde by Leonor Fini, 1948

She unconsciously emerges out of blackened waters,
among automatic drawings of curious eyes.

Would she be wearing only pink silk cardinal's stockings?
Would she prefer to walk alone? She disturbs the air

as a dark swan, ready to sit in a chair made out of a corset
she would never wear. The world collapses at her feet.

What barrier does decomposition have on this unearthly water?
A woman like this defies men and inhabits the intense.

What dark waters do you drink? Seduction like this is not for the
weak. Where does the end begin and the beginning end?

She is the earth-mother, the dangerous angel, the merciless lover,
the caution we throw away and embrace.

Martin Willitts Jr.

MEASURING DEGREES OF LONGING AT THE METROPOLITAN OPERA HOUSE

i. Intermission: On the Grand Tier

I reached into my pocket today
at the Metropolitan Opera House,
and discovered a strand of your hair.
How do I explain that I, in that moment,
fell more in love with you?

Can it be measured in degrees?

They're ringing those bells again
and the woman on the balcony
in the pink, silk gown
is considering whether to gulp her champagne.
I'm not moved, I love the sound of the bells.
Ushers, priests and butlers all get to ring bells at us.
I'm thinking now that loving you is the sanest thing I've ever done.

The woman on the balcony is leaning forward slightly,
Perched on her vulnerable wrists,
Facing the fullness of the day
and the great crystalline abyss.
Her Romeo is relieving himself of coffee and bourbon
And she is posing half-consciously
awaiting his return.

I'm thinking now that she is as lovely as she will ever be in her life:
The midday sun celebrates her face.
In the cool, marble shade her cheeks are two roses.
I'm thinking now that,
In this moment,
She reminds me of you.

Yes.
Don't think it so cliche'd,
Momentary longing
Becomes
Enduring
Desire.

ii. Lunching with Placido Domingo

Wrapped in your mother's scarf I'm content with loving you.
I'll have to wait for lunch today,
And when I do sit down to eat left over pasta
I'll have to pick out the figs.
I don't care for figs in my pasta
and It's cold in the back of the store.

I'm supposed to be on lunch break
but I thought I might first digest a morsel
of Sidney Portier's book given to me for my birthday.

Wrapped in your mother's scarf I'm content to just
Look at the cover,
Into his eyes.
Here's an envelope for your letter my love!

Would your mother mind if I said,
"I'll love you forever"?

Placido Domingo's face looks despairingly at the wall
from the poster over the manager's desk.
Something on the stock shelf has troubled him.

Wrapped in your mother's scarf I'm content to stare
at his muddled face:
the black of his shirt reflecting gold light
Making him immortal.
In the cafeteria,
his gray, thinning hair,
Stubbled chin and arching posture
stopped my breath short.
He seems to grow old in secret.

On the subway
I ran into an old acquaintance,
a stranger really.

I felt embarrassed
not to be working at the Public,
for not being invited to the Tony's,

for not being remembered.

I was proud to be thought of as
something possibly resembling a Yalie,
for having an agent,
for having also met President Clinton.

Wrapped in your mother's scarf
I feel proud for having kissed your mouth.

On the train I feel the sun nudge the back of my neck,
reminding me of your nose on my cheek,
Your closed eyes meeting mine, saying,

"Beloved".

Kenyon Adams

THE STEPS NEVER LIE

To dance with you,
      to twirl you,
to fold and then unfurl you
      like a flower beneath the sun.
Maybe romantic,
      perhaps enchanted,
      but charmed, nonetheless,
          and one.

Simply to smile,
      softly to laugh,
to write both finally and draft,
      like a fantasy yet to play.
Maybe be cautious,
      perhaps call the shots, but
      please,
          don't run away.

And the steps intertwined
      like a painting,
          like vines,
      to climb their own path to the sky.
Softer than clouds,
      intense, but not loud,
          think of then,
              drink to now,
'cuz, Shannon,
      the steps never lie.

Evan Dunn

HANNAH

Our parents packed up a 1953 Ford station wagon with seven children, and enough clothes to last for two weeks. Destination? Funk, Nebraska, in the middle of almost nowhere. That little spot on the map could just as well have been called Fun, Nebraska, because it's where Hannah and Owen Jones lived on an expansive farm, carved out of the Nebraska landscape. My grandmother came from Swedish stock.

When I close my eyes, I can visualize the final stretch of our westward journey. We usually arrived after dark, but we all screamed with excitement as we strained to see a warm, soft light coming from my grandmother's kitchen.

We might have been looking at a farmstead, seemingly in the middle of nowhere, but to us, this was a wonderland. Across from the sturdy house sat a large barn. We spent hours in that place, constructing elaborate passageways and forts up in the hayloft. If a person wanted to, he could hide up there and never be found.

Collecting eggs in the morning provided its own excitement as I did my best not to get pecked by the hens or to drop any eggs. In addition to corn, alfalfa, and wheat that grew on the farm, Grandpa Jones also kept horses and cattle. But there was one section of his land that he never tilled. There he showed us buffalo wallows and the tracks of pioneer wagon trains, still cut into the soil.

My grandmother provided delicious meals, using an oven and stove that burned corn cobs. Water was hand-pumped in the kitchen, and the bathroom? That would be the outhouse in the back yard. I remember being horrified the first time I saw her cut the head off of a chicken. The bird wrestled out of her hands and ran across the farmyard before it finally dropped to the ground. Up until then, I thought chicken simply came from the meat section of a grocery store.

Because of the many children in our family, our grandfather built a swing in the barn. Long ropes were attached to a beam and connected to a sturdy board for the seat. And there was no end to the exploring we could do around the farm, inside several smaller out buildings, and grain bins.

My grandmother would rise early in the morning, getting food ready for the Anderson clan. Her strong faith, commitment, and love permeated everything she did. When asked if we could have some special kind of treat or dessert before we left, her answer was always the same, and spoken with a smile, "You shall."

As I think back, I'm struck with the many lessons I learned, each time we visited that farm. My grandmother demonstrated that hard work is rewarded. Life may be difficult at times, but it's worth the journey. Hannah was gentle and cheerful, no matter the circumstances. She taught me to be thankful for what we have. And when blessings come; be thankful.

Max Elliot Anderson

THESE ARE THE DAYS OF GROWING SHADOWS

these are the days when shadows can't hide
these are the days of the blinding light
feet fall softly in the cool cool green
you make me laugh until it hurts
race to the water and run right through
so much time and so little to do
help me eat these sweet tarts
help me watch those clouds
hide with me in the magnolia tree
we tangle up so earnestly
fall asleep while the world blurs past
wake up warm and completely confused
then it's time to tear ourselves away
leaving me with that terrible feel
your many mysteries seem to heal

winding down mount vernon road
red dirt on my white gator shirt
a little pain but nothing hurts
it's all everything, everything good

then the days of the growing shadows
these are days of the golden light
when our footsteps start to crackle
while we're busy making other plans
so little time so much to do
pack up your mom's old wagon
knowing the time just makes it worse
something lodges in my throat
now my room only echoes of you
i rev my engine past your house
but you aren't there to hear it
half roll of sweet tarts on your porch
you aren't there to share it
i'll go to where it says i have to
walk through all the hallowed halls
and wait for the glorious day
when we'll run, cool green under our feet

Bill Kowalski

GLASS GLANCES
For Sylvia Plath

I can return from this
I will return from this

Take your rivers of blood
Your oceans of salt

And bury them with
Your head

Art imitates life
Art is never life
Life is life

If life were art
We would all be dead
Victims of our own deadly crimes

Keep your buckets of beef
Your refrigerator of tar

My oven is for pizza
And sirloin steak

Not fragile egos
And broken promises to myself

I love
I love
And I fear not the repercussions
I hope

Radomir Vojtech Luza

HOPE

Even when stuck in one place,
you are a dancer.
There is movement in your heart,
your, spirit explodes
the way flames move
on the log ballroom
of a fireplace.

When you feel without,
I will never lose my hope
in you. Even when you
hang on, like a white birch
swaying crazy like a metronome,
the storm passes and
you didn't die on a bed
of plush moss, I know, you
still grow even if no one else
sees the world
in trees as I do-

understand that you become
higher and higher,
where even the weakest of twigs
still dance in the rhythm
of the wind, each winter
their spring buds
stretch to the sun,
a progression now bigger
than you, in a forest dwarfing
the people left standing,
reaching up,
in the darkness.

Timothy Gager

MOSTLY BASIE WITH A LITTLE BACH

Whenever I see a new woman, I know
I should look at her hair and her eyes and her smile
before I decide if she's worth the small talk
and the dinner later
and whatever else she may require
before she becomes taffy,
pliant and smiling.
But that never works for me.
Whenever I see a new woman,
what matters to me is never
her hair or her eyes or her smile;

what matters to me is her saunter
as I stroll behind her.
If her moon comes over the mountain
and loops in languor, left to right,
and then loops back again,
primed for another revolution, then
I introduce myself immediately
no matter where we are,
in the stairwell or on the street
and that's when I see for the first time
her hair and her eyes and her smile
but they are never a distraction since
I'm lost in the music of her saunter.

Years ago, tall and loping Carol Ann
took a train to Chicago,
found a job and then one summer day
walked ahead of me on Michigan Avenue
while I surveyed her universe amid
the cabs screeching, horns beeping,
a driver's middle finger rising.
Suddenly she turned and said hello
and we shook hands and I saw her smile
dart like a minnow and then disappear
as she frowned and asked
why was I walking behind her.

I told her I was on my way to the noon Mass

at Holy Name Cathedral and she was welcome
to come along. The sermon wouldn't be much,
I said, but the coffee and bagels afterward
would be plentiful, enough to cover lunch.
And Jesus Christ Himself would be there.
She didn't believe me, not at all,
and she hasn't believed me since.

That was thirty years ago and now
her smile is still a minnow
darting here and there but now
it's more important than her saunter
which is still a symphony,
mostly Basie with a little Bach.

And I no longer traipse Michigan Avenue
as I did years ago looking for new moons
swirling in my universe. Instead,
I take my lunch in a little bag
on a long train from the suburbs
and I marvel at one fact:
It's been thirty years since I first heard
the music in her saunter
and Carol Ann and I are
still together, praise the Lord.
Who can believe it? Not I.
Carol Ann says she knew
the ending from the start.
Lord, Almighty. Fancy that.

Donal Mahoney

OFF FOR AWHILE

off for a while she goes
with another version of this life
a platonic parallel that gets this sophist taken to task
plenty of flights and flying off
after the bookmark at least
suggested a tear in to and near the center
of that second hand paperback republic
one you have toyed and flirted with
when boredom bothered
when appearances aged and altered
when curiosity piqued/peaked again
 desperation constricted from the inside and out
looking across a dust settled clearing
rains and a second half twilight chill set in
with an outgrowth and pouring over pride
brought one odd and two even sweet seasons

off for a while today they go
on a larger, charitable stroll
some benefit to masses
rather than one intimate stranger
for an affliction that took her
early by the hand
but once on at least three occasions
this scribe who hashes out
a little something for a small public's indifference
was hers , one or both
cause and affliction

Mark Radseszewski

THE RISE AND FALL OF KAHLIL GIBRAN

They shuffled by,
matching waif like tortoise,
waddling along
in heavy wool grey overcoats
holding on
to each other's arm
as does the vine
to molting mortar.
Breath of Listerine
pungent in the air
smiling their contentment
made me have to ask...
as I simply had to know...
what could be the secret
in the beauty of
their unisons while
dawdle dancing home.
Kind sir, I beg of you,
impart on me your wisdom please
your length of vows
tell me now
tell me how
you've managed
all these years.
Stopping in his tracks
ignoring me minutely
for but a moment more
he bent and brushed
with gentle lips
his beauty's
bright red blushing cheek.
Inseparable appendage
sewn to his side
she was there
forever, against the rising tides.
Then, and only then
he turned,
and through the trials
of a million miles,
he looked into my eyes and spoke,

"My son
Kahlil Gibran,
he got it wrong!
The oak and cypress tree,"

then gently shook his head,
"Too far apart
allowing light
sneaking in-between
enables roots to
get their hold
and soon from
seeds of discontent
where once were
dreams and confidence
grow
weeds to intervene."
You see, he said
continuing
his long labored soliloquy
"We've never been apart,
and thus the soil
'neath our feet
has never seen
luminosity.
Nothing there
will germinate
to rise and
come between.
"But what about the pillars?"
I asked in
utter disbelief.
Could he really mean
"Kahlil Gibran,
the 'exalted'
whose words,
the spoken mantra,
has always been the wisdom
far beyond reproach?
"One need only ask Delilah
about the reality of strength.
When someone finds

themselves between
two pillars set apart
leverage will seduce them
to tumble man made marble
make it crash unto the ground
But pillars, sitting side by side
solidity, in monolithicity
allows nothing
in-between

and thus
will weather any
storm or rumble
that comes from deep,
far beneath
this very sacred ground.
Lest you
doubt my words
today,
then let me add
into this, my interminable dissertation;
that a single drop of water
deep in crevice crack
when turned to ice
will leverage like
a vice at vulcrum's point
and move once proud
and mighty peaks
becoming little more
then pebbles
lying far below
upon the valley's floor.
Heed my words
should cracks
appear
fill them quick
with all your heart,
and seal them with a tear.
I've learned a lot
these many years
and thus I say to you;
stand firm my son,

stand fast,
against all that comes your way
stand very tight together
till yours and hers,
breath and beat,
harmonic tangencies
so closely drawn together
that one plus one
shall be compelled
to always equal one!"

G. Thomas Edwards

SNAPDRAGONS CRACKLE

Snapdragons crackle
in the air for Maura
and her flowing gait,

a swagger neither Nora
nor Maureen would ever
let a suitor savor.

Maura knows
that in her wake
men with scythes

and burlap sacks,
creep like gators,
eyes afire, jaws agape.

Nora and Maureen
can smell these men.
Unlike Maura

and her flowing gait,
Nora and Maureen will smile,
take their time and wait.

Donal Mahoney

EVENING WALK

Main St.

We stroll past guinea pigs running
treadmills in a plate-glass window
--we'd rather fuck

Almansor Park

We kiss on a concrete bench,
watch ducks float like boats
in the placid man-made lake

Almansor St.

Our streetlight framed
shadows stride hand-in-hand
up the cool sidewalk

Don Kingfisher Campbell

TREMBLED EVENING

Cross street has always been her favorite street. She takes the bus four or five stops past her stop every day after work because she likes to walk down the cracked sidewalks and touch every verdant lawn. This one has a privacy fence, thin wood slats painted green with peach trim. She can see the floral wonderland beyond. This one has a large bush that looks like a fluffy mound of shaved ice. This one has a hedge with leaves large and softer than her hands. She hi-fives them as she walks by, shaking off sweet drops of water.

The bright grayness is almost strange, as if the sun has melted and become particles of soft woolen light floating around her in the mist that turns everyone into wet-haired ghosts.

Her favorite is the Gemini tree. It is nothing special, nor is the house it guards, but she loves the vision of twin trunks sprouting from one under-earth acorn for centuries more. She looks up at the leaning twins, seemingly wanting to embrace her like a tall, caulicle mother. She envisions their death: one of them gets sick and in the storm-night's violence the weight of its dying body brings them both down.

Near the end of the walk is the silence park. It's a tiny park, tucked between a cul-de-sac and a parking lot. She seeks sanctuary in this sacrosanct lot, but a man who lurks beyond the wall that separates her stronger self from the shell that once was shocks her with his presence.

He's come to ask for forgiveness for leaving her with their dead child. Without speaking, the grass sighs under the weight of his remorseful career laden with forsaken sins. His choices are dark barbs that gossip about their own demise, flagitiously unwilling to accept inferiority to this meager being meekly approaching their master. With angular elbows at his waist, he holds his arms out. A force stronger than gravity pulls her shaking chin into his muscular neck. She hears the rending wound of betrayal vibrate from his esophagus into her colloquial ear.

His weakness released her and his hands hurry to hide the gash in his pig-bled stomach, which she created with her bright steel anti-rape blade. At first it seems as if one of his carcass-devouring intestines is trying to escape, but what is witnessed is his death hole giving birth

77

to a Gemini tree. He is flattened to the ground under its life-bearing weight. He begs to scream against the sprouting honey-suckle pushing his eyes from their sockets, but a vaginal-shaped rose bush rises from his mouth. His penis turns into two soft silky vines that sprout hand-sized leaves. She walks toward home as the emerald whisper-snakes climb high into the milky air, wrapping themselves around those that will never part, while the lullaby she hums echoes through the trembled evening.

Jason Maul

"When I see a pretty girl walking down the street I think two things. One part of me wants to take her out and talk to her and be real nice and sweet and treat her right, while the other wonders what her head would look like on a stick." – Ed Gein

HOOKED

The hook slicks in.

How easily she snags.
How tightly she tugs.

She knows no surrender.
Long in exile, she returns,
To lead you to forgotten rooms.

In a careless moment
She sucks the tongue from your mouth.
Coils it round your demon need,
Slips it back behind your lips.

You swallow her hard.
Scornfully, she sniggers at you.
Knows that you can't do without her,
In spite of your painstaking
Hopeless attempts.

She washes over your mind like an old friend,
With the comforting allure of a new lover.
And she's back with her pedicure
In the ring of your desires;
Your powerless soul at prayer
Under the Gothic arch of her painted foot.

Arne Torneck

WOMAN IS NOT A FLOWER

fragile nature
of raging hormones
drooling volcanoes
keep it in bed
throw away
all keys & keyholes
pillow fight
we never agreed
on anything
but silence & leather
except a safe word i
forget the safe word
stop no ok
funny the way
you can get younger
try to please the pain
a child will believe
anything you teach
them not to see
to believe in a L-ve
a love with a name like G-d
afraid of you i am
love is all you know
you answer to no one &
nothing higher than
your heartbeats &
your libidinals
unhand that cradle rock
hurt & heal me now
you have all the power
you feel so good
about yourself
how is a girl like a flower
how is a boy like a knife
there is birth right
for equality we fight
tomorrow like yesterday
you put a smile
on my face
undress me with your

dress off
you throw like a girl
i lay down my gun
in your apocalypse
last day of
being careful
what you fish for
stick out my neck
stick out your tongue
who loves
the other more
hurt me more
hear me roar
every potentiality
every capability
every fragility
fast forward to now
i dream i die i write
a thousand deaths
doth not make a coward
a woman is not a flower
a woman is not a flower
imagine the power
you kiss your mother
with that mouth
anything you can do
i can do good
you love me best
you love me better

Vox Anon

AURORA'S OPIATE AUBADE

You're a fucking drug—and I'm addicted.
I'm jonesing for you, babe, like methadone:
mu cure, verve, velvet illness all in one
sterile syringe; my pleasure-pain, inflicted
intravenously, freebased or smoked.
It's the same shit. Your potency retains
me more at risk each time these servile veins
strike gold in your fire—shattered, smoldered, stoked

at just a touch. You: waifish heroine
of doom; unkind, trim bud of my demise;
the callous weed choking out my heart. It hits
like unrequited—fuck!—the way your eyes
turn hazy. You're not gonna let me in.
My soul's getting the shakes. Come on, just one more fix.

Scott Miller

INSULATION

Oh baby, you were
so out of control,
falling out of your
dance dress
under a narcotic
evening moon

You thought
you still had it together.

You screeched red terror.
I thought your heart
would tear open right there.
So loudly you roared
"I don't care"
and at that point I saw
the switch to your wits
shut down its current.

That's right
you didn't care.
You didn't worry about
the confusion of uppers
or downers

You didn't lose sleep over
thoughts of dehydration
impending starvation.
So quickly,
like a sponge out of water
your In Style body
became dried flesh.

Now you sprawl on cigarette butts
and dried chewing gum
stiletto heals
awkwardly side-steps
your skeletal frame,

you've doubled your pleasure

alright,
—right onto the streets.

Counting days backwards
your lights dim,
your eyes become two hollow storerooms
insulation as thick
as the buildings around you.

Electrical conductors inert,
spark incomplete,
flashing recall

champagne flutes
pills by the handful
cocaine lines jump-cutting
to crack pipes

and the sad faces of former friends
—caretakers held hostage too long
by your ruin.

Ten Sunday mornings later,
corner of Cahuenga and Vine
newspaper man hawking headlines.

Drooped across cement lines
your dancewear
smudged and greasy
panty hose shredded
and caked in homeless grime,
heels busted.

Corroding like the handle
of your rusted vanity mirror
you clutch a Styrofoam cup
full of coins
from Samaritans walking
toward their redemption.

Church bells thump
in the distance.   Jerry Garcia

COFFEE MANDATORY

Just so you know... I never planned to fall in love.

It started out as nothing more than a relationship of convenience. Like sex for a green card or the wash of a windshield for a couple of bucks at a stop light in Santa Monica. A fucking transaction. No emotion... no feelings. Just a need meeting another need. No romance, no flowers... just the glare of a naked bulb at sunrise, and the grunting of guilty pleasure heard on the other side of a thin kitchen wall.

After a while, like with any illegitimate relationship... and enough lying to yourself in the mirror... eventually you decide that maybe it's okay to take next step... the *public* step. A coffee house. The thought was innocent enough in your head, "It's just a cup of coffee. What could happen?"

Until you get there, and you wonder if this is how they feel in Amsterdam... ordering heroin... in a brothel.

At first, there's that self-conscious thought that goes, "people don't really do this in public... do they?" Followed by a second thought that you should just go finish your business in the restroom like the upstanding citizen your parents always thought you'd be. But you stay... you take your seat in the big room with all the other upstanding citizens... and you lose yourself to the overwhelming urge that brought you here in the first place. To take this private need to the next level. So you do. In front of God and everyone... if only God were watching.

I never planned to fall in love.

Years pass, and things go on like always. Public meetings, intimate rendezvous, long mornings after a bad night's sleep. Every encounter making you sink deeper and deeper into what was such an innocent addiction. Days and nights became the same to you. Multiple jobs, endless hours... and only one thing remains the same. The need. The intense need, the unsatisfied need... the aching need.

Until another comes along.

As the glare of the naked bulb at sunrise still calls after you like a line out of a song by Mumford & Sons, the something new doesn't *call* like a selfish bitch... it whispers softly in your ear, like the one that got away. It draws me to a softer place... a darker place, later and later in the night... after the glare of day, and all its distractions, goes away. And unlike the whorishly obvious coffee brothel, it is subtle and almost... caring. And the scars of years are replaced by tender strokes to a raw-rubbed ego. The only thing required in return was to think, and feel... and write. And whatever words came out were good... were accepted. I was accepted.

I never planned to fall in love. Not like this.

More years pass, and things change... drastically. The flutter and surge of my heart, gentle ego stroking... the sideways-smiles-turned-lustful... change. Flutters turn to questions. Surges to pain. The lying, sideways smiles, with their promise of fulfillment... turn to insistence. And whispers turn to ice at the harsh dawning of a new day, when I know it has become... the same.

I look up from the computer. I see the light of morning enter through the fog of early June. "When did this happen?" is all I can say, in a hushed voice, raw from not speaking. I turn my head the other way, toward the kitchen, to the glare of a naked bulb at sunrise...

...just so you know.

Bill Friday

STIGMATA

Phoned my friend on Christmas Eve, we hadn't spoken in a while. "Is Mary there?" "Um ... no ... she's not ... she died about a week ago ... a Prozac, booze and Demerol O.D." Went to the tavern where I'd found her, where we often sat and talked; ordered us two ginger ales (her drink of choice was ginger ale). The drinks arrived, I raised one glass and clinked it to the other, knocked mine back, and left hers bubbling flat atop our carved initials in the bar. Went home and thought a lot about her: only girl I ever heard mix hockey, Kant and titty-fucking in a stream of conversation. Thought too, about the onion skins of scars that ringed her forearms; how she wore those slashes brazenly, like bracelets of cheap jewelry; while showing off her puckered flesh at every opportunity. Wondered how she'd felt when she performed her bloody magic: did she need the searing slits, to know the passion of her pain; was there a numinous release; or did she simply need to mortify, panhandle some affection. Wonder got the best of me: I took a razor to my wrists and opened up the skin. Not much: two tiny crying crosses draining from my mortal flesh, that's all.....................................

Arne Torneck

THE NIGHT OF THE CRAZY EYES

This was not the night
my head went through your windshield
and I apologized - from breaking it.
This was not the day - your car exploded
and we dove out of a rolling fireball.
This was not the night - I talked myself out of a bullet.
No - this is the night of the crazy eyes.
The night I dodged jail and everything that followed.

This is the night of a Bellingham bar-crawl
That night - I encountered crazy eyes,
our verbal and non-verbal interplay went on for hours -
building toward merged-flesh promises.

But I heard whispers of instinct - "extract yourself."
"Do not run - wild things will case you down."
I slowly did the dance of retreat - even as I mentally
caressed and undressed every curve of her.
Picturing hours we could spend till daylight arrived.

That next day - she was in the news.
Raped - Battered - Sliced - Slashed.
A bloody mess the reports said.
The professor - that man she met after me -
took her home - becoming guilty.

The Universities' woman's groups circled the jail -
called for his flesh - condemned every man.
They had their martyr and
a poster-boy for their fears and hatred.

A few weeks past - then the truth.
She had spent time in a Tennessee sanitarium.
Had a history of self-mutilation.
Of pounding her head and body into walls.
Of eating sympathy of those who rushed to her aid.
He had dropped her off - no more.

The truth laid bare - silence - no retractions.
No apologizes for defamation.

A career over - A life scarred by implication.
Just silence.
All men are guilty - sooner or later.

Duane Kirby Jensen

TRACK MARKS

It was a hot summer afternoon in 1998 when I found myself once again at the doorstep of my drug dealer's house in Canoga Park, California. I had been up for two days on crystal meth and was drenched in LSD. My pupils were so dilated that my eyes looked as black as death warmed over.

When I entered the house of perpetual euphoria, I saw that the usual gang of misfits and cretins were present. They were all slamming drugs into their veins and giggling like a deranged pack of school girls. I knew I was in for quite a ride when I saw the remnants of a VCR had been taken apart and re-arranged to look like a metallic chicken. I sat down on the dirt encrusted, puke green sofa and glanced down at the 80's style glass table in front of me. A huge white line of meth stared back at me and I knew I couldn't wait any longer for the rush. I pulled out a glass tweeter and lit the end with a shitty dollar store lighter. Once it was red hot I snorted the line and felt it melt into my lungs as I blew out a puff of smoke like a medieval dragon. The drug hit me fast and hard, I felt as if my skin was ripped from my body while a shotgun blew the top of my skull off. The burn from the meth destroyed my esophagus as dripping mucus raced down my throat.

While my dealer was busy trying to molest some thirteen year old girl, I walked around into the back room, and there I saw something beautiful. A young woman, maybe 18 or 19, curled up next to a destroyed mattress. Her hair was cut short, dyed crimson red, and was greasy from the amount of product in her follicles. She had track marks that marched up her arm like a colony of fire ants, and dark circles that rested gracefully under her pale, blue eyes.

I felt a gush of warmth shoot through my system and decided to chat with her. She spoke in a drug induced stupor that turned me on. Something about that voice of hers was quite alluring, but I was too high to have sex at this point, so my admiration of her was more out of the cold and disturbing beauty she held deep within her soul. I gently touched her pale, white skin with my blistered fingertips trying to feel something real in my life. She reminded me of the one that got away. That young girl from my past that had moved so far away, leaving me aching inside for something more. Was this the girl I had been waiting for?

After an hour or so of the basic, boring getting to know you bullshit conversation, I knew it was time to get her out of there. My drug dealer was a predator, and he wouldn't be satisfied until he got her so strung out that he could strap her to a table and force her into a gangbang with his fellow creeps. When we got back to my house, she decided to shoot up once again, because the sickness was creeping in and pretty soon she'd be vomiting all over the place. I watched her inject some meth into what was left of her veins, and I snorted the rest of the drugs left in the cellophane of her cigarette packet.

I pulled out my watercolors and a small paint brush and asked if I could paint her portrait. She agreed, but wanted to pose nude. Of course, I had no objection to this, and the heat was rather awful by this point so I decided to disrobe as well. After the drugs filled her system, I saw her face light up and a fresh beauty shone through her that seemed magical. I tried my best to paint, and at the time I thought it looked great, but upon sobriety the painting looked like something out of a kindergarten art project.

After painting her picture and chain smoking some cigarettes for awhile, we eventually passed out from sheer exhaustion. When I woke up later the next day, she had disappeared. At first I didn't care, since I was in miserable shape myself. The drugs had left my system and I was in desperate need for water and hydration. I crawled across my carpet and made my way into the kitchen and was able to get a drink. I could feel the cartilage in my bones falling apart and I needed to get high immediately to release myself from the pain lurking inside. Luckily, I had a hiding spot underneath my dresser for occasions such as this. After a quick snort, I felt alive again and made my way out into the blaring sunlight. I searched the apartment complex for the girl but found no trace. It was as if she had never existed, but I was convinced that she must have gone back to the dealer's house to score more dope, but he claimed he hadn't seen her. I bought some more meth from him and retreated home like a soldier returning from a cold, nasty war.

About a week later I heard rumors that a police raid was on its way to the apartments in our area. Paranoia hit me hard, and I knew there was enough evidence of drug abuse in my house to have me locked away for the rest of my life. I quickly threw all of my paraphernalia, and any evidence of illegal narcotics, into a small trash bag.

As I walked out to the dumpster behind the apartments to toss out the remnants of my personal debauchery, I smelled something rotten escaping from the large receptacle. I looked underneath the layers of trash to find out what the hell that vomitous smell was coming from. Upon closer inspection, I witnessed a most disturbing sight that destroyed the very fabric of my existence. It was the girl! Her corpse had been shoved inside the dumpster like a discarded children's toy. Dried blood crept out the corner of her gaping mouth. Her teeth had been smashed out of her gums and her fingertips had been clipped off. She was barely recognizable in this state as flies buzzed around her and small, white maggots crawled out of the pores in her skin. Her eyes were yellow and staring right at me, and I felt sick for a moment before I regained my composure and quickly covered her back up with the numerous trash bags surrounding her.

I knew what had happened, she must have overdosed over at my dealer's house and he did what any lunatic in his position would have done. This was nothing new in the area, since people had been disappearing on an almost daily basis for years. I remembered a few months prior, when a buddy of mine got paid big bucks to dump some human remains over a cliff in the hills of Chatsworth. This, however, was a world I was used to, and the sacrifice for normal living to fuel my drug addiction was worth it in my head at the time. Still, I will miss that girl, and the small amount of time we had together. I will always think of her fondly within those little moments we had in the midst of insane drug use that shatters the mind and spirit into oblivion.

Chris J. Miller

PRINCESS OF THE BROKEN VOW
AT MT. NEBO CEMETERY

Curtains closed on sparkling Miami nightlife
Strange youth overcomes me
Calls me to visit Mt. Nebo Cemetery

Grampa Sam the bookie
Buried beside Grandma Ida
Who made the juiciest hamburgers

Grandpa Harry the loan shark
Buried beside Grandma Ethel
Who died of insulin shock

And Dad, an attorney and real estate developer
In his polished granite loft

The unmarked slot beside him
Reserved for my asthmatic mother
Who always wanted to be a sculptor

And 100 feet west of my blood
A suicide, Lindsay, my first love

O, Princess of Broken Vows
I'm here again
With your inconstant bones

To see what nightmare goes walking
Through geranium, hibiscus and oleander

To revisit silky oils and perfume
Patchouli, French powders

Mascara stains on tear soaked corners of
A goose down comforter

You call me back to the panic of a new moon
Our last Coconut Grove reunion

After a college rendition of *Hair*

We drove back to my flat
Fell inside each other

Music deepened the senses, deepened confession

You flailed for possessions

Boys were leashed
But you couldn't sort out Truth
From imported shoes, stuffed toys
Or costume jewelry

When tremors racked your body
Wealth pulled you down

Now plastic flowers adorn your epitaph
Mt. Nebo 3 a.m.

Dad's reddened ears
A man and his Scotch
Elbows on the wobbling bar of
The Embers
Orating off-color jokes
In a highbrow circus of diamond mirrors
Crystal chandeliers

And Lindsay, you were always there
Just a few deaths away

From my father's bad heart
Floating beside me

Under mother's fresh quilts
The gentle pause of your hand
Over my thighs

Clouds danced

A zodiac of rooster, rabbit, bagel and lox

We pulled our bodies closer

Condensations of stilt-rooted islands
Blue jeans pushed hastily to bed's tight tuck

When a tropical storm came up
Stripped coconuts from the trees
And the trees bowed in supplication

We said it wasn't *really* making love

Then with black angry eyes
You taught me about broken vows

With suntanned boys
Who flew south for the winter
From New Jersey or New York

Lies and seduction
That was only the beginning

The heart lives with lies
And dies with compromise

On my knees at Mt. Nebo, 3 a.m.
Where Father drunk and proud can hear me pray

Where my Princess of Broken Vows lies
Between bays, crystal skies, palms and pearls

Where the body belongs to no one to hold too long

Michael Rothenberg

GOD DUG A SHALLOW GRAVE IN MY HEART

God dug a shallow grave in my heart to bury your face in
but I could still smell your skin
It clung to my mouth
stuck in the corners
on my mind
your lips
their taste
through the dirt
your breath
down through the years
tickling the belly of my wrists
across my eyelashes

We shared a kiss
between the ticks
to put it all behind us
we held hands
lay still in a beam of time
we comforted each other
slid the world from each other's shoulders.

You can't bury that.

Hart D. Fisher

SYLVIA PLATH

You remind me of Sylvia Plath
All tattoos and nose bleed

No nonsense
Blue bubble gum

The nectar from your bosom
Drowns the lion's head
And the tiger's tail

For in the end
You are invisible
Like a metal mule
A white raven

The reason for
Reason's fall

Into the ghost yard
Of guilt and gas

Bordering design's disgust
With the blue beauty
Of your breath

The very children
You swear to believe in
Slaughtered at the shore

The dream you
Divide and multiply

Forgotten after
        The feast

Radomir Vojtech Luza

I HEARD HER CALL MY NAME

When I was 17, I used to live with a girl called Linda. That was a time of jeans and T-shirts - still my favorite clothes for a woman. Linda didn't dress like that. She always wore a dark green dress, rather formal, with pockets that I always wanted to slip my hands into. And with this she wore Irish shoes too. - black, a little formal, with rounded toes and high square heels.

This was a share house - myself, Linda, her boyfriend Ian, and John. The others were junkies. These were tough, dangerous men, but I didn't realise that at the time. They were seldom home, and on the weekend they would go out, knock off two or three chemist shops and return with a heap of goodies. Dope, too. Ian would visit his grandmother in a country town, come back with about six bags full of freshly-cut marijuana, dry it in the oven and the house would reek of fumes.

Since we were alone in the house a lot, I came to know Linda. No romance on either side, but deepening respect and friendship, long discussions on art and philosophy. Her dark blue eyes looking out at me from her ruined beauty, her junky's cheeks already sunken and her skin beginning to turn bad. She told me she used to inject under her tongue, so that her arms would remain clear. I suppose she had never found anyone with whom she could talk about the deep things that moved her soul. And I didn't know it but she thought of herself as lost, already damned, and to her, she was looking across a fence towards something that she felt had gone from her life forever, if indeed it had ever been there.

One night we were sitting at the low wooden coffee table. She'd hit a charity for free food that day - ten bags of chips for dinner. There was a syringe on the table, and I knew the boys recently brought home a load of tablets so I asked to try it. She stopped my arm by clutching at my wrist and turned to me.

"No," she said, and tears started in those dark lost eyes. "This isn't like the other drugs. This isn't the way for you. This drug is death. It is death. You're a good person. Don't go that way." And that is how I remember her, frozen in that pleading moment, leaning forward, looking intensely into my eyes.

Many years afterwards, I was told that Linda had died - no details. And then I remembered a dream that I had about three years after I moved out. In the dream, Linda was calling me by name, though I could not see her and did not realise who it was until after I woke up. She was calling for help, and she sounded as if she was in terror. And then her voice got further and further away.

Thomas Kent

NIGHTS WITH ELI, NOW PASSED
for Eli Coppola

a fierceness in the eyes
piercing into mine
with an honest
gaze

she talks soft with an
emphasis on fragility
in awkward moments
we share with some
medicine to calm
both of our illness
but cure nothing
in between us

we talk words and writers
'til early in the morning
she says she is finally
tired enough to sleep
in spite of the pain so
I leave her a big bud
and give her a kiss
good-bye as I roll
out into the early
morning cruise
down to 16th
and Mission

I feel like a coward as I
cook up a shot in the
Eula Hotel and I count
every step it takes to
climb up to her place
as the dope runs into

my heavy mind and it
all gets a little lighter
for a moment and I
have hope that her
condition will change
but it never does
getting up to her
pad gets harder
and harder
for her

then for me
regret is not so bad by the balloon
or remorse so effective by the spoonful

she invites me over and I lie sometimes
when I am weakest and she never seems
to care, but I know who I am and I drink
to her when she passes and the whiskey
tastes like acid and it burns a memory
into my guts of what I could have been
what I should have done, but didn't
crying as I hung up the phone instead
her memorial is the beauty of her words
that I feel so undeserving of

she never left me without a smile
always told me what was on her mind
she spit in the face of demons that I ran from
I kissed the mouths of the angels that cloaked her
they held her so tight that she could not walk away
from a fate that was never a deterrence to her spirit

she loved skid row poets and donut shops late at night
she loved music that you could dance to and songs that
were sung off key with a wink and a sparkle in doe-like eyes

she loved me even though I could not love myself enough to
give her love back when she asked for it, never demanded it so
I went where angels looked away to get her voice out of my head
because her kindness seemed wasted on my broken life

she left a hole that wings won't let her walk back through
after a decade away from this she still enters my thoughts
she tells me cool words arranged like staccato messengers
and delivered with proud timpani rhythms and beats as
I bring her back to life in dreams and listen to her ask for a
joint, but if not that, maybe a cigarette

she is the smoking angel of my memories that puts ashes
in my eyes
I still love her madly for her passion that she injected
into my heart
like hot heroin that I craved to quell the riots of fear
that she
was never afraid of as she brushed my matted hair away
from my temple and hushed me in her shaking arms

we spilled wine and laughed and she never judged me

or ignored me
in crowded bars of drunk poets or from across a pillow
we shared for the night
she made the most inappropriate jokes about
crutches and sex as
we lay naked together in the clean softness of her bedding
when she died from a failed heart it broke mine in a silent
hidden spot
that no one ever saw until today, when the words named it
and I cried
her named out loud and alone

then I smiled as I felt her coo back from the darkness

and my fears were hushed once again
I never lose her words or the place where our
souls touched
she is there in the sunrise on her street looking out over
china basin as it glints like mother of pearl
at the start of
another San Francisco day

another day without her struggling to tell me something
with me hearing nothing but the song
the song in her voice that is
a song of simple love
a song of simple friendship
a song of simple kindness

she tells me without struggle
in my best dreams where
she makes deals with
an afterlife that
I won't have
alone
not if she
can help it

A. Razor

LOSING MY BEST FRIEND TO HEROIN

The rosary hung from
your rear-view mirror
exploded, the beads
rolled down the crease
of the vinyl seats
as if they were
headed down a drain.

Your Hail Marys and Our Fathers
are forsaken now,

You won't be saved.

Timothy Gager

MEMORY OF A BLUE CERAMIC ASHTRAY

Last time I saw you
we sat in our favorite
shoreline restaurant
underneath sporadic
formations of seabirds.

You broke a blue
lacquered fingernail
smashing out your
Marlborough Light
while cursing me.

The maitre'd called
a cab for you.
I finished my Chivas rocks
paid the check
and left alone.

Sundown rested
behind midnight blue
waters of sharks
and other cold blooded
creatures.

Headlights animated
hedges and mile markers
on the nasty bleak highway
edging Malibu's ocean cliffs.

In my Spanish tiled flat
under the Mexican Fan Palms
of Venice
sleep came easily
closing my eyes
on your final image:
grainy gray ash
red stained cigarette butt
blue ceramic ashtray.

From - Askew, Issue #11
Jerry Garcia

IT HAS NOTHING TO DO WITH US

It has nothing to do with us

It has everything to do with tattooed lips, suicide prevention,
dragons, cross bones, red stars & sacred hearts. It has nothing to do
with us. It has everything to do with pool halls, Irish whiskey,
Coca-Cola, the house rules. Local boys grumble, lose quarters
in the juke box. Spoons of cappuccino froth at closing time
in the Blue Danube Cafe. The Danube the nearest body of water
when Narcissus and Echo go to town

It has nothing to do with us

It has everything to do with abstraction, connecting lines in a story
written as it was meant to be written. It isn't chance. It isn't. It's
sky, dance, eye staring into eternity. It has to do with mouths,
fingertips. Radio loud up singing. Romantic truth. It has everything
to do with youth. Trees. The ones we're imagining. Not those old
oaks we saw claw spasmodically in noon heat, branches drenched
in green lichen. Fence stumps grown with moss, horses in corrals.
It's got to do with morale. Everything to do with something holy:
Calistoga, 1992, blue sky day. Mineral springs bubble in the motel
swimming pool. Discovery of neck, hands, hair, and foot. Madam
Dora, tarot reader, palmist:

OUT TO LUNCH

It's got nothing to do with us

We're only dust. It has to do with stopping the sun. Half-naked on
a beach before the prom. Photographs of who we once were.
What do you think of me now?

It has nothing to do with us

It has to do with remembering to forget our desires because they're
too painful. And because they're too beautiful we're afraid to run
far. We turn tiny circles around suburban yards. We forget. It has
everything to do with things we try to forget. The faint groan,
the whispered cry of much *too much!*

It has nothing to do with us

It has everything to do with stepping away from burning lips,
burning the fringe of everything around us

It has nothing to do with saying yes

Or the smell of us. Or kissing the neck of a disembodied lover

It has nothing to do with us

It has everything to do with impulse. How it burrows through
melting snowfields of our last night. Flushed, you wave goodnight.
Lower the drawbridge to your cliff-side house. It has everything to
do with a mouse inside our throats, quivering a whisker to find
a clear note. Coming back to ourselves. While the mechanism of
the cosmos fails. Evolution skips a beat. We retreat!

It has nothing to do with us

It has everything to do with lust. Coursing through our bodies,
shot-full. Thy Kingdom Come, this falling down, rapture on the
come. Chrysanthemum. Narcissus in clay pot beside a rose bush

It has nothing to do with us

It has everything to do with all we've seen, heard and felt

It has nothing to do with us

Dogs yelp in the woods, hungry on a hunt

The huntress mired in quicksand...
The arrow never lands

Echo turns to Narcissus
Is this who I am?
She wants to know, before the bog suffocates her

The boy offers his hand

Echo asks, *Does this love, death, have anything to do with us?*
She takes his hand rather than wait for an answer

Narcissus, never very good with words
grips Echo and murmurs
It has nothing to do with this
He lifts her from the bog
It has everything to do with moments unresolved
Everything to do with us. It must!

It has everything to do with this. They kiss.

Michael Rothenberg

WARM SALT

I bet you thought I'd catch you
I bet you counted on it
Like so many times before
And I tried; I did

But you kept falling
And falling
And falling
So many times...so many ways

I begged you, pleaded...please
Please stop!

But it called, and once again, you answered...
Looking at me through glazed eyes,
Sweat and blood
I pray when she gets older,
She forgets seeing you like that

I can't believe you'd forsake us so easily...

You missed the first day of school today.
She was so brave
As she entered the door and looked back at me,
All I could see...was you

She needed you there...and tonight,
She asked if she could-
Go sleep with mommy, "under the ground"

How am I supposed to answer that?

Just like so many times before
I am left to clean up your mess

I'm trying love, I really am
But God, I hate the flavor of
Her tears

Kevin Craig

A MOTHER'S LOVE

She chews up her
own breasts
Rather than suckle me

She puts me on a pedestal
So I can't escape her whip

She pinches me under white linen
And dares me to cry – or she'll kill me

She smashes me against temple walls
And splits me apart like ripe fruit

She takes to her bed and swallows her drug
And slides me a portion to hook me

She rakes away what's left of my skin
With the metal comb of her ten red nails

Yet, I hasten back to her
Broken and bloodied
Since she makes me believe
She's the only one who'll love me

Arne Torneck

BATTERED BEHIND DARK GLASSES

An otherwise beautiful lady
with eyes matted and closed
is not exactly sleeping.

The trouble goes deeper,
the doctor has a laser
light drill penetrating her eyes
that have turned thunderstorm
black with smudges of red and pink.

She tells herself this will never
happen again, there will be no
rebirth with him.

In idle hours she self-nurses
a cave of hurts. The lights are off;
her eyes are bruised and burning.

In the morning, still in bed she looks in a mirror,
Her face thickened with puff and irony-
she weeps splinters sounds.

Above her head on the lamp desk the alarm clock keep ticking,
across the room, around the corner, the refrigerator keeps humming.

The man who had his way is dark in her, like distant echoes
embedded in a memory or shadow.

She owes him nothing. He hears none of her sounds.

Michael Lee Johnson

RIO

It's always a her
a she
from across the room
across the void
someone I trusted
beating me down
tearing me up
ripping me apart when things were too quiet

Rio
with soft sighs
liquid brown eyes
melting the wall
softening the blow
hitting me where it counts
where the secrets used to be
where I'm soft
deep between her thighs
hitting me down low
where no one else would go
licking out the wounds
eating the dead flesh
hungry for something fresh
something hers

Rio
beating me
'cuz I look so pretty when I cry
my face so tender when it's wet
she promised with an embrace
lied with another angry glare

Rio
my best friend
my undoing
my rocket into dirt
face first
mouth dry and filthy
but I'm still standing
with a lightning bolt in my chest

a brand glittering to someone sheltered
I get back up every time she kicks out my legs

Lips split and swollen
I get up off the ground
out of the grave
her every lie dug
her every kiss laid out
I get out of her grave
I go looking for more
more pain
more ambiguity

She's sorry
she didn't mean that
she was tired
she had a long day at work
traffic was a bitch
the boss is a prick
her ex-boyfriend needed her
a bad acid trip
he kept her up all night
she didn't mean to hit me
someone gave her a white rose

She didn't mean to say that
all class
No
really,
she trusts me
until I'm out of sight
out of body
out of mind

Rio
my best friend
my worst enemy
her face tells me everything I need to know.
she will settle
for nothing less
than our mutual destruction.

                                        Hart D. Fisher

ZAFADA

Skinned - we slide and merged in and over
one an-others bodies - two explorers mapping
our way through unknown territory -
two hungry mouths tugging at flesh
they way machetes fall bamboo - extracting salt
they way some suck marrow from bone -
catching-then-releasing darting tongues
they way children play with fireflies -
until you said, "Hit me." - "Hit me hard."
My passion retreated - the noise of the world
reclaimed its place within my room
at the corner of Garden and Chestnut
within the late-winter of a Bellingham morning
and I was back on Earth.

"Hit me in the face. Hit me!" she repeated
showing me her closed fist.
Words - lost within my throat -
I shook my head no - no - No!
She read it in my eyes "Zafada"
Her blues turned black - she hit me -
full fist-ed in my face - then again and again -
then she was pounding my chest and arms
two pistons gaining speed to nowhere
until her rage burnt out - the way
wildfires die after consuming all that is consumable.

Exhausted - she crumpled into tears
that turned my belly into a lake -
her head buried beneath small waves -
hoping - I believe - to drown herself.
With the quietness of wind stirred to life
by hummingbird wings,
she asked, "Why didn't you hit me?"

Duane Kirby Jensen

WALTER'S PERFECT WOMAN (SHED'S OUT BACK)

A lot of weird things can happen inside an old shed. Such is the case of Walter Burmwell, a forty year old, unemployed electrical engineer. You see, the older Walter Burmwell got, the less interested he was in sex.

As a youth, he was a real womanizer, spending much of his free time hoping into the beds of free-minded youths, without a care in the world. Those days had passed and Walter's beer gut proved it. No more of those glorious days in the sun where young girls went skinny dipping in the lake and Walter joined them for a frolic. Now it was more of the same garbage day in and out. Walter had never settled down with a woman, so he spent his spare time pining over lost loves. He had tried using those internet dating services, but alas, the dates were always a failure. He would go out to meet these woman, only to find that he had passed them in time. He was out of touch with the youth of America, and just seemed like an old fart to the woman around him.

Walter still watched VHS tapes, listened to CD's, and played board games. He never evolved with the revolution of technology, so his house had the feel of a museum to it. Sure every now and again, he would meet some nice lady on the internet, only to find out when he met them in person that they were at least two-hundred pounds overweight. Walter knew he had to do something. He could no longer live this lonely life, and deal with the disappointments of women. So he decided to make his own.

Walter started stalking various females over at the local yoga studio and at Ned's Classy Hair Salon. These places were brimming with young sweaty flesh and Walter had a devious plan indeed. During his formative years at the university for electrical engineering, he had seen dead things twitch with the right amount of power. In his daze of psychotic thought processing, he thought he might be able to build his own woman out of electrical parts and human limbs. At the very best, it would be the world's most sophisticated blow up doll.

Cathy was the first to go. He waited until the sun went down and darkness filled the night sky. Walter grabbed her screaming from the parking lot and threw her into the trunk of his car. Cathy had a great body, with strong thighs of steel, but her face left much to be desired, and Walter was a picky son of a bitch. Walter also didn't care much for her silicone breasts, he thought they looked goofy and fake, which was not his preference. He was a fan of flapper-jack tits, that sagged and drooped around the ribs.

He took the body into the small shed in his backyard, where his most crazed fantasies became a reality. After chopping off Cathy's head and discarding the mammary glands, Walter decided to go to Ned's and wait for another prime victim. Kirsten had these wonky tits that would be perfect for his creation, but once again, her face was not even close to his liking. In fact the more he thought about it, he really didn't need a face at all. "Why not go headless?" he thought to himself.

After sewing on the new breasts, Walter clamped off the stump of the neck with a metal lid. He thought it would help keep in the smell from the rot of the body, but alas, this didn't work very well. Walter spent a good six months trying to bring his creation to life, but all he could get it to do was twitch constantly. For a while this worked for him. He would turn on the machine and the dead body would flail around on the table, and he would have deep intercourse with it. He could feel the electricity flying around the body, and it tickled his testicles in ways he couldn't comprehend.

Then the body started to decompose, and the flesh on the body started to peel off like cooked chicken skin. The muscle tissue underneath seemed to almost melt away from the bones, and the stench was getting worse every day. Walter decided to have a final go with the mangled corpse, before discarding it. He was pretty drunk that night, but he screwed his brains out with that thing. However, the rum glass he had set next to his feet, got knocked over in the midst of his orgasm. The rum hit some electrical wiring and Walter was fried like a bird on a power line. The alcohol mixed with the massive amount of electrical current also caused the corpse to erupt in a huge flame. A gigantic explosion occurred sending pieces of Walter, his shed, and the pieced together body throughout his neighborhood.

Police were baffled when they arrived at the scene. They had no idea what exactly went on in that shed... But we know... don't we...

Chris J. Miller

NOD IS NEY PRINCESSES

like me
pretty on the inside
yet ugly beast seeking
princesses that like
running away being
captive &/or comatose
woken by a kiss no
sugar spice everything nice
sex we eat died in eden
harmless dolls hysterectomy me
hosts parasite eve complex
a cult of unpink & very ungirly
the evil of the man
rainbow skinned girls
from around the world
deepest desires fears he
stealing & selling you
your dreams demons
ethnicities identities
epitomes modesty
paraded pageantry
outsinging birds is
pretty safe yes
no ambitions no aspirations
but to kiss a prince
happily ever after
comes never closer
to heaven on earth
than the horizon
then below your navel
spies secrets sleepers
witch hunts why
which one are you
the prophet or the peek a boo
unblamed & monolithic virginal
refinement so young too innocent
new mutual empathies sulfur
post men syndrome suffer
symphonies affections
confectionately

yours silences not
violent enough
unspoiled appeal fair skin
blonde hair no mirror mirror
little ones volunteer
for blonde lobotomies
pretty on the inside
fertility goddesses
gross anatomy marry me baby me
equality in an man's world no
damsels never in
need of rescuing
dragonizing your
distress undresses
stockholm syndrome & feminazi
here we go poor self images
self hatred id ego super ego
my unteachable peach me the man
who sold the world i am you
free me of cherries &
1850's feminists are sexiest
fairy tales hundreds years old
reimagined retold & SOLD
virtue admired only
for her beauty kill your family
her unselfish sacrifice
her fans will sing along
friday friday fun fun fun
popstars do not rise they fall
she calculated my weakness well
to rule the world precosmic &
protect pricecheck preorgasmic
architect branding children
lifestyles looks vultures
IDEALs private invites to
shave your privacy innocence
shed your man for
the cartoon mouse for
this poem is looking phallic
for everything but the girl for
initiation rites gone wrong
circumcision & clitorectomies

1 cut removes the hood
covers the male genital organ
the other amputates a greater
portion of the female organ itself
to secure masculine privilege
the other acts to subordinate women &
place their sexuality in
service to plastics & populating
world patriarchies nations
kissing bang bangs to armageddon
leave your daughters alone
plant your manmade
sinstruments instead
build new edens without
mirrors perfecting
perfection appraising true
beauty & invisible attributes
like equal & challenging stay
speechless sublime & ineffable
there are nod is ney princesses
there are nod is ney princesses
there is you human
not divine ruling from
an unbroken maternal line your
homogametics to adolescence on
uniquely born & made are you
asking me or telling me woman i
heart you i love you i love
the you you are
pretty on the inside
pretty on the inside
like me

vox anon

"The true man wants two things: danger and play. For that reason he wants woman, as the most dangerous plaything." — Friedrich Nietzsche

ATTACK OF THE FIVE FOOT WOMAN

I watched her
wolf trees

Saw her
slurp plants

Gasped as she
sliced off heads

Glazed because
she cracked
open shells

But she didn't
devour me

Invited me instead
into her cave

Don Kingfisher Campbell

VICTIMLESS

she is the noisy girl
who will never
shut up

she
no one can tame
not even
with a gift

I am the man who would
try to feed that beast
whatever it wanted
just to see
what she might eat next

A. Razor

FEW HARD WINTERS FROM EXTINCTION

Your adventures
Always bigger, wilder

I invoke satyrs and your nymphs
Bang hollow trees with stolen Puritan clogs.

I can't match your magic
Your she wolf descent on a fenced in herd.

I've dedicated my last fun to you, hoping
My kill will lure you from your den.

How laughable:
A kid with a pellet gun could claim the bounty on me.

But you have a shaman tracking you, wanting
Your ears as pedants, your green eyes as sparkle

To sprinkle on the melting snow.

M. Frias May

THE ABUSE OF VENUS

The swooning redness, scabby wells
wounded woman, for this you would suckle the babe
and let ripen – grow fat, abject ideas of love
till the blood dries and it is scrubbed clean in private
while your family watches the monster sleep.

Jayson Pida

THE FAMILY TREE

Bill Johnston was sick and tired of his angry, manipulative, and self-righteous grandmother. She owned the house he stayed in and was always on his case about one thing or another. Both of his parents had died when he was a kid, and he spent his teenage years growing up in this hellhole. The house was decorated with creepy statues of the mother Mary and all the saints. She prayed to them every night like some kind of insane idol worshiper, and shrieked fire and brimstone passages at Bill, for the most ridiculous of activities.

For instance, she caught him eating a Mr. Goodbar one night and she beat him mercilessly for indulging in the senses. She found him listening to a radio station playing a rock and roll song and smacked him in the face and called him the devil. His problems with woman were even worse as he was so twisted he had never even kissed a girl. His grandmother had him convinced that they were all harlots with diseases, so Bill stayed away from them out of fear of getting AIDS.

Well, when he turned twenty one he had had just about enough. One night after a long day of his grandmother screaming at him to get a job, he walked into her bedroom with a shovel and bashed her face in with it. A flash of blood misted through the room like a shroud of red smoke. He chopped up her body into small, tiny pieces with a hacksaw and buried her in the garden in the backyard. Since it was right before Christmas, he had one of those three inch ciprés de Lawson (European tree) and took it out of the pot and transplanted it in the dirt where she was buried.

"That bitch will make good fertilizer." He said to himself.

Bill called the police and told them his elderly grandmother had wandered off and he couldn't find her. It was a big city with many missing persons cases and they seemed uninterested to say the least. Bill hung up the phone jumped in the air and felt a joy unlike any before in his life. Now he could do all the things she wouldn't let him do, and after a few months of her not turning up, he would inherit the house and her money.

As the years went on the tree his grandmother was buried under grew and grew, eventually hovering well over 10 feet tall. But as the tree grew fuller and rich with life, Bill grew old and gnarly. He spent many years indulging in every debauchery a man could do, and it showed in his face. Although his grandmother was a religious fanatic, some of the things she said turned out to be true.

"Beware of the evils of sex and the Babylonian whore!"

One of the first things he did after killing her was hire an escort for the night. The sex was amazing and he felt great, but a week later he found out he got the clap and was pissing razorblades for a week.

"Drugs are evil! The Devil in disguise!"

Bill tried smoking pot, but it made him uncomfortable and paranoid. He tried his hand at booze, but only got sick. He tried crack and felt destroyed after the high wore off. He even tried mushrooms, but had a terrible trip and thought he would never return back to reality.

"Eat fruits and vegetables! Fatty foods are for the gluttonous sinners."

Bill stocked up on frozen pizzas, hamburgers, hot dogs and pork rinds. Within six months he had gained 80 pounds in his belly, and had no energy during the day.

"Pornography will rot your brain and turn you into a pervert!"

Bill spent so much dough on porno movies at the local video store that he was running out of his inheritance money fast. He was renting ten to fifteen videos a night! He eventually had to quit renting pornos and get himself a job.

Bill couldn't help but wonder; why is it that everything that feels so good in the world, so destructive to one's own life? Was his grandmother right about these things? Were they really sins? Or had he been so deprived of these things as a kid that he was just overdoing everything?

Bill's mental facility started to disintegrate and after awhile his paranoia became overpowering. Late at night he would hear the calls of his grandmother's twisted voice calling upon him to clean up his act. The sounds drove him mad, and he felt as if the whole world had finally caught on to what he had done.

In the midst of his insanity he walked out into the garden and stood in front of the tree. He could see his grandmother's face inside the bark mocking him. He went to the garage and got himself an axe, and then walked back over to the tree and started cutting it down. Looking like an insane lumber jack, Bill cut through the wood intensely. He wailed and shouted throughout the night, until the tree fell to the ground. He threw his axe on the grass and wobbled back inside his house.

The next morning he woke up and decided to take the dead tree and throw it in a dumpster somewhere, far away from his home. However, when he walked outside he found that the tree was still there, bigger than before, by at least five more feet! In the tree he now saw thousands of those pesky faces of his grandmother, barking and sneering direct orders at him.

Bill had had enough. He walked into the garage and grabbed some nylon rope. He walked back over to the tree and stared at it for a moment. He then threw the rope over one of the branches and drew himself a noose. He duct taped a note to his shirt and hung himself over his Grandmothers grave. The note read: THAT CRAZY BITCH IS BURIED BENEATH ME!

Chris J. Miller

FIERY SHANNON

Once I met a fiery Shannon,
     a heart like steel wool.
She takes a thousand degrees to melt,
     and as many hours to cool.
Always afraid she's abrasive,
     though a sweeter voice I know not.
Though she may give frozen stares,
     the fire inside her burns hot.
Never too careless, she carries her heart
     like the highest-bid piece at an auction.
Should you step to her too boldly,
     she'll give a glare and a bit of her caution.
Once I met a fiery Shannon:
     soft like a warm, Spring day,
     stubborn like a firing cannon…
She quickly blew me away.

Evan Dunn

SALLY STONE BURNS HER BOSS

On a chilly downtown day, in a springtime bleak
pipes were freezing all around, it rather was a freak.
People walked on sidewalks dry, and onto black ice glass
and should they slip, well that was it, they froze right on their ass.

Now Sally Stone, she was a clerk, up at the town hall
her boss, he was quite the jerk (in line for voodoo doll)
but Sally filed and Sally typed, and also gave good phone
'though never enough for her bad boss, as on and on he'd drone

"Type up my notes, fill in the blanks, you know what I would say.
You know that I'd be mayor, were it not this lame toupeé.
Sally where's my blazer, and my signet and my tie
would you make me coffee pleeze, you need to zip my fly????!!"

His requesting ran her ragged, his requests just made her mad
But on this chilly downtown day, she'd finally taken all he had.
So when he asked that she see about the heat,
She drenched him in some bourbon, and strapped him to his seat

She piled him up with shredded briefs and bits of chopped up desk,
then struck a match upon his zipper, and lit the blaze grotesque.
His toupeé was the first to burn, like a marshmallow on a stick
(expanding with a blackened skin, then melting in a slick).

His blazer did amaze her with its flames of green and blue
then popping golden sparkles, that came off of his left shoe.
His belt was quite a fuse as it sizzled and it fizzled,
then exploded at the buckle, as ash fell down in drizzles.

His pants were fried, his shirt was toast, like breakfast for an ogre.
Just pass the salt and butter, add a side of heinous bogers
But the man himself just would not burn, and nor would he talk
All he did was sit and grin, while Sally only gawked.

When finally his lips did part, he cried hot tears of steam
"where have you been all of your life, you are a lawyer's dream
"I think that I don't pay enough, for you are worth much more.
"You owe me a new hair piece," then he stood and crossed the floor.

"Now clean this up, type my notes, I've appointments yet to keep"
With that he shut his office door, as Sally wept and sweeped.
Outside of the townhell, the ice did fin'ly melt away
And became to most who saw it, just another day.

But Sally Stone knows different, from her part as fire's voyeur,
And the flame's that would not burn her boss, a devil of a lawyer,
And every year thereafter, on the calendar she'd gaze,
She'd sigh, and smile to herself, about the time she got a raise.

Daniel A. Armstrong

A WARM GUN

She's a shotgun
blast of a woman --
abundant force,
very little precision.
Where she hits
she draws blood.
At close range
she blows holes in things.
But when she misses
her metal screams
itself out, falling
sans effect,
like a brief hard
drizzle over forest
and field,
shrugged off even
by the skittering wren.

Rob Dakin

LOVE-38

Love
isn't always clean, happy, or bright
for one man it's excuse to kill
for another reason to die
and in between, a thousand men say
"Love you? Married you, didn't I?"
So what gives us the right
to so much happiness,
silliness, laughter, joy?
We say so, and
in the shared dresser drawer
a loaded .38

Wyatt Underwood

GRITTY

"I don't like your poetry" She say's
"Too Gritty!"
And fucks me with her tongue -
Golden flecks in her eyes
hypnotic.

She grips my buttocks with
crisscrossed ankles
tearing into my back with her
filthy nails - there's blood.

She wrings my insides
pulls her dirty knees
up for depth and smiles.
She holds the back of my
neck tightly.

"your poetry - brat boy
is shit -
far too

Gritty!"

Roger Cornish

134

HAYZEL

The gorgeous girl who's bored of being
  beautiful, adorns her Cleopatra eyes
    with black mascara, not to justify
  herself to any Anthony, but to assert
    her dominion over her own body.
The sharp, dark features of her face
  lay hidden under paint and piercings
    and her hair like two ravens taking flight
  in opposite directions. Stretched and torn,
    her shirt's so worn, you can see right through her.
She blends in with the darkness around her,
  and like the moon at daybreak, wanes to a sliver.
    The next time you see her, she has left her lover,
  and in a final bid to reinvent
    herself, she razorblades her head.
Her hair spills like the evening sky
    across her neck and marks her for her own.

Matthew Nadelson

CONSONANCE
for dear friend and fellow poet Constance Stadler

for one moment
arm in arm,
gazing skyward
(who knew that stars could
actually form a canopy?)

for one heartbeat-optional moment
bathed in twinkling chastity
we lived wholly within each other,
you and i –
perfect friends,
god-given

for one resplendent,
montane midnight moment
we held
one breath
in two bodies
beneath Orion
with Philotes smiling down

for one unstained moment of divine grace,
twin exhaled awe-spirals danced
a November paean

for one immortal moment
(that one was enough)

agápe
was ours ...

Rich Follett

BE-ALL

to kiss
as if there was another word
tongues searching for that other word

words, ways
to describe this –
tongues, far from foreign
foraging for exquisite illustration
illustrious forays

to kiss
such that outside eyes
are out of operation
for longer than it takes
to have a deep bath
or lunch with a friend

third eyes press like
the pad of sated panthers,
moving this way and that
at the sway of soft brows

to kiss
not foreplay
the be-all meeting of mouths,
of faces, of hidden eyes
admission to hidden selves

the selves we surrender only
when communion is brought
in acts of consummation

yet with lips, only lips
end-all lips

Luke Prater

SHE IS

she writes to me softly
and moves so gently

she
  she
    she

leaves me speechless
making me feel as though I could
never write a poem deserving of her smile
she leaves me with no option,
but to say the simplest things:

she is beautiful
she is unforgettable
she is lovely

she is the reason I can't sleep

she
  she
    she

she writes to me softly
and moves so gently

she
  she
    she

is Alicia

Taylor D Mackintosh

A WAFT

In like a fragrance
I never saw you coming

Now you're inside this mind of mine
And I can't truthfully say
If what you're doing is nice
But I like it

It's like bees to pollen
It's not romantic; this is pure attraction

Turning potential into action
Your gaze into the whole of every fraction
Bringing us back to this thing about ransom
Because in like a fragrance
You won't let me go

You're all that's on this mind of mine
But rewind and find just why we get into
The same situation we're always
Getting ourselves into, out of
Through, and around

Because even now, as we bounce
We're still one step behind gravity
And even then, as we bounce away
We're another step behind relativity

And figuratively speaking
You're what's in this sight of mine
But more than that, you're what's in the lenses of every sense
And I'm tuning into you and your mannerisms
Because your intentions are silent
But so close by
So I fight through this room, cutting down the dead
Because just for you, I'd do anything you said
Because everything you've said was once just a word
And every word was once just a breath
And when you sweetly released it
'Hello' I finally was able to hear you

To breathe you in

And as I looked up
I was able to take in your visage
And when I did
I tasted the immediate memory
Of this wish

As your fragrance kissed my lips
You became everything
Need is made of

Inside my head, I hear my green strings being strung instead
Do you hear me singing through the static?

If you are
I get the feeling
When you only hear my exhale
You will know everything left unsaid
When I say nothing

In like a fragrance
I never saw you coming

Jason Brain

THE UNLIMITED ORGASMIC POTENTIAL OF THE HUMAN FEMALE

you make something kinda go
SNAP
in there
a mind bends only just so far
then
I
becomes
It
that's the point where
(if you're a selfish bastard)
you can claim The Prize
but if
  if
if you're
a nice guy
a friend
a teacher
a healer
a good person
then
is when
you free the trapped bird of her soul

she'll come back

Steven Sassmann

KINDLE

I love
How you kindle
The horizon
On my way home,
Firing damp hedgerows
With the undressed caress
Of wistful memory,
To turn my wheels
To careworn tunes,
To forget the hours
That haunted our gap,
To guide my feet
Unbroken to yours.

I love
How you trick
The moon
Into your pocket,
And smuggle it
Into our house,
Just to light it
On the hearth,
To drive the chill
From russet cheeks,
To numb the torment
Creeping beyond the door,
To let the flames
Pipe us to rest.

I love
How you charm
The snakes
Of insecurity
To dance
Like children
Lost in time,
To keep me from
Faithless silence,
To bewitch darkness
With the laughter of Gods,

To remind me
That meanings grow wild
When the sun ceases.

I love
How you conjured
Nourishment from spoil,
And set it
At my table,
So I had no choice,
But to eat,
To enjoy,
To smile,
To love you.

Nicholas Vaughn

SATELLITE LOVER

Satellite Lover set me alight
Give me one hour before you take flight
Give me the last key to your room
A place on your bed and the taste of perfume
A violent cocktail I'll be taking tonight
From the curve of a glass to the curve of your thighs
Wrapping around me in a boa embrace
Arrow tongue poised, expressionless face
Taking me places on every street where you stand
An odyssey of lust
On every bed where we land

Satellite Lover set me alight
Free me from this ecstasy
Destroy this appetite
Until I've had my fill of you
Let me violate that space
Tear out the very part of you
That's given me the taste
Then lover let me look at you
With your swollen eyes of tears
Biting back the emptiness
Of all your lonely years
With the payment of a stranger
I hold out my hand
And you clasp it for the danger
Where your twilight world is found
Cutting deep inside of you
Measuring your soul
Poisoning every part of you
Subtracting from your whole

Then hastily I withdraw from you
Like an assassin's guilty knife
The satisfaction bringing me
Once again to life

Spencer Slater

144

HOW TO HELP A WOMAN REALIZE SHE IS BEAUTIFUL
WHEN SHE FEELS OTHERWISE

You can't just say "You are beautiful",
       unless of course she thinks you are pretty sexy, too.
Compliments always have more weight
       when they come from someone we esteem.
But if you share my misfortune of not being particularly desirable,
       that simple statement might get through
          with added emphasis:
"You are *beautiful*" —
       like speaking in Italics.
But this is futile if you have used it too many times,
       so try something new, try something that rhymes,
          or just a different word:
"Gorgeous, dazzling, lovely, stunning, hott — with two t's"
       But at some point her heart will declare
          "I have heard
             it all."
English fell short.
So I looked up all the synonyms for beautiful
       in Hindi, Spanish, Arabic, Indonesian,
          and Sign Language,
       and still did not feel like she
          was adequately conveyed.
But whose fault is that?
How can words do her justice,
       when even pictures struggle?
"You're just saying that."
       The infamous last resort.
"You don't mean that."
She is cornered,
       she cannot run away anymore;
you're getting close —
       too close for her comfort.
So flank her defenses with her favorite flowers.
       No note.
          No words necessary.
Just a metaphor.
       Beauty begets beauty...
          so she gets these.

But if you're broke,
      and really busy,
and poems keep turning up pathetic,
      and posies and pink roses seem pitiful,
and her circumstances are unchangeable,
      and date nights didn't do it,
      and after all your conversations about how
          society's standard of beauty
      is severely screwed up,
she still hears the lies about her body,
      and you've tried naming every detail you love,
      but in her eyes, every argument is frail,
and intimacy gets tense,
      and each compliment seems a pretense,
and your admiration of her
      has no chance of defeating
          her expectations of herself,
and if you had one wish
      it would be to trade places,
      to understand,
and then stand in her stead,
      bear her burdens on your head,
and regardless of how she looks,
      she still looks the best you've ever seen,
      and that doesn't even make sense,
but she may never comprehend
      what you mean;
after you have tried everything to get past these walls--
      scaling them, breaking them down,
      going under or around;
once you have bled prayers for her sake,
      bred fury—not at her—but at the brutal hatred
      of a culture of men that will bury her
if it means they can have their way,
      and having spent day after day hoping to carry her
finally off of the battlefield,
      but knowing fully that you are no rescuer,
      no knight-in-shining-armor, no savior,
then... wait...
grieving each ounce of fearful self-doubt
      dropped like slavery on her shoulders...

wait...
      knowing
she *is* ethereal reality so fantastic
      even she thinks it must be fantasy...
wait...
      begging God to open her eyes.
Dreams will only feel unreal, darling,
      until they are simply realized.

Evan Dunn

WOMEN

Women! I'm bound to listen to them, heed their words and obey them.

Look at me and my mother: it never occurred to me to act beyond her purview. I wore her tyranny like a wetsuit. Nothing could intrude between me and it, and I never really peeled it off. I'll be buried in it.

It works the other way, too; my observance of feminine fiat. Look at me and my wife. Though she allows me the illusion of my efficacy, when it comes down to it, I'd no more go against her wisdom than bite off my tongue. She just knows. I don't. I need her to help me make my way in the world. This is not an exaggeration. I know myself. And everything in between; from barristers to bimbos, I need and heed them all.

I did some grocery shopping yesterday. I settled the amount with my debit card, and remembering out loud the hair-cutting appointment I had made for that afternoon, asked for forty-dollars cash back.

"You don't need a haircut you look beautiful," said the woman cashier. "Thank you," I said; and told her I'd go straight home and cancel the appointment. Which I did!

Three women live in my house, five if you count my wife and the cat. My wife is rarely home, though, and the cat is but a cat. The three women I'm referring to are visa students, visiting Canada to improve their English. One of the three, an Iranian woman and I were talking yesterday when I decided to go watch the news on TV. She told me how much she disliked TV, and I told her that I didn't like it either, that it was just a bad habit for me. "So, don't watch it," she said. "I won't, then," I said. And I didn't. I told her that that was the second time I had heeded the advice of a woman in a matter of hours. I proceeded to tell her about the woman in the grocery store.

When I got to the point in the story where the cashier said, "You don't need a haircut," I made a snap decision to leave out the compliment that followed. I thought it would be superfluous vanity. "You look beautiful," added the woman from Iran, filling precisely the space of my deletion.

So, why wouldn't I listen to women? Why wouldn't any man heed their words and obey them? When they tell him he looks beautiful?

Arne Torneck

IN MY EYES

by day,
you'll fuss at your shape
fend off my praise
accuse me of flattery
scowl at the mirror
dread the stare of the scale

in pale night,
I can admire you
without a debate
I won't wake you
from your transcendent serenity
my moment of reverence
you bring music to my silence
the purity of your breathing
its slow and rhythmic cadence
frees me for reflection
on your Stradivarius curves
the plushness of your rear
a treat for a man's eyes
the melodic lines of your belly and breasts
harmonize with panes of moonlight
your voluptuous mouth
the gentleness of your eyelids
your hair resplendent and dark
so gloriously thick
arrayed across your neck
so inviting to my lips

your tender state
precious in slumber
beauty in tranquility
barely restrains my ardor
scarcely quiets my wild desires
lightly holds the leash
of the feral side of me

who wants to tear your clothes off
kiss you hard
bite your shoulder

suck your neck
squeeze your nipples
pull your hair
hold you down
spread your legs wide
slam against you
set loose the beast in you
make you howl with me

but for now, I am quieted
my fury is at bay
for now, I'm at peace
pleased merely to adore you
stretched across my bed
delectable and sinuous
long and lyrical
innocent and sensuous
in your effortless magnificence

everything a woman should be

Bill Kowalski

CELESTIAL SPHERES

The ripened roundness
of a lavishing
sm o o th
female breast
unacknowledged
by the proper
who would chuckle
at Columbus'
unflattened world

JR Phillips

FOR NINA SIMONE

with every mistrusted minute
intolerable loves break out into an insufferable song

the hapless gasp of what cannot be
runs through every conduit of light and dark

to place the impossible jewel of the impossible love
into an impossible crown

betrayal beckoned
blackened the blackness
liberated the hatred
sung the sweetness
for nothing
for hopelessness
for you who were you
lastly
alone

and the crowds came to cluster around your piano
around the dulcet venom
around the unforgiving anger

applaud the queen
applaud the goddess
applaud the diva of soul
high priestess of intolerable beauty

lost child in life's mayhem
loved by her voice

which the populace could never hear until
they placed rhythms to it which never should have been

plastic close ups beat the fragrances of spring kisses

who can still smell your lament

as the mass weep before heaps of hideous flowers

for the dead they can't remember
for their dead friends who live in their salacious minds
programmed to erect eject reject

yes my dear

so it is
they have no heed
your voice hopeless
from a land yonder
unwelcome here
where dreams of nonsense rise
in collective orgasm
exchanging artless loves

o the incompetent lovers

they were not worth it

whoever was you never met
or never trusted
or never sung
the echo of your mutual becomings
lost and misunderstood forever in
this diminishing land of lost souls
where love cannot be
where the winds are the objective complement
of the highest angers caressed by God's finger
where History spoke hushed crushed
as your piano
as your black bird
as your Porgy

as you

(for Nina Simone)

Dom Gabrielli

A BEDTIME STORY

Give me the wild from yesterday's fury
Give me a while to gather my speed
We don't have time for a bedtime story
I know what you want
And I know what you need
And I may not be wiser than stories of old
Which you've heard all before
As the sheets unfold
Whilst I'm writing your part
As if for the stage
In our bedroom theatre
Where lovers engage
In one to one combat
Before we retreat
Catch up with our breath
And relentlessly proceed
To prolong every second
To be longer than the last
In the arch of your back
I'll know that you'll cast
Yourself to the part
And your purse to receive
Every bedtime story
I've ever conceived
In the depths of my mind
Rescue me now
Help me find
The reasons how
You came to be here
Across my bed
Naked and Waiting
Like a book unread
I long for those words
That you weave
Like a spell
The suspense, the mystery, the thriller
You tell

Spencer Slater

RISING

the rising of a woman
(as she grips the day)
from the beach
from the dream pillow
her freckles
her toenails
her itinerant motherhood
the pain she wears like a shawl
the cocktail dress celebration

her laughter is a kite hanging over the waves
her sad eyed beauty the wind
the sun a corsage for the universe

and she
rising
rising through all of this
through
despite
because of all of this

she grips the day
in her love drenched fingers
in her angry teeth
in her supple eardrums
she grips the day with inevitability
with unique rhythms
with unerring accuracy
she grips it with beautiful mistakes
and phyrric victories
eyes open and stunning

as she grips the day
(the rising of a woman)
she takes hold of life
with fists like sieves
detritus falling away
palms filled with amazing

David McIntire

WHAT YOU TAKE

you look at me then with eyes like small moons
you touch me and my body is charged with stars

what falls from your waist fuels my hunger
your toes' red-painted blessings paint my heart

there is a bird singing in the barren tree limbs
and a hawk flies over the revelation of my breath

and you have taken them into your small brown palms
like petals of an orchid red purple and blue

Charles Smith

GLOBAL WARMING

I love to
put my nose in
the black hair waterfall

I love to
swim in the pools
of her eyes

I love to
kiss the soft land
that is her lips

I love to
trace the peaks
about her shoulders

Run my hands
down the slopes
around her sides

Then I go
back to the start
because we're in public

(Later I will love to
lick the flower
between her legs)

Don Kingfisher Campbell

MORNINGS WITH YOU

The glitter in your hair
Has lost its sparkle
The morning air
Feels so brittle
What shall we do today?
You say
Without hope or thought
We could just lie here and smile I say
Everything seems easier that way
It's never wasted by your side I think
but the words don't come
and I lie there in silence
and smile

Dexuality Valentino

POSTURES

I remember how you washed my feet
as Christ's prostitute had
bearing the burden with expensive oils

but I am not protected from your agitation of my heart
nor the experience of your witness
around corners or in coffee shops

what little we have to say is not spoken
conferred by looks, glances and gesture
teenaged postures of mutual affectation

Jhon Baker

MAKING SOUP

I split a pea pod into strips
as my lover unzips her jeans.

I spill two peas, ripe and supple
as her nipples, into the iron pot.

One holds fast to the folds of green skin
that sheathe the little clitoris within.

Coiled in the corner of her room,
we ball in our sleeping bag womb,

slipping wearily into the sleep
we knew once in our mother, buried deep

in the recesses of her flesh, and plucked
from one wet world to another.

Matthew Nadelson

HOW IT HAPPENS

The first thing any young romantic needs to know
Is that hearts will be broken

The second is how to survive
A broken heart

It starts with a glance
Whether with the eyes
A scent, a touch, an essence
And continues on

And from there
It spirals into a few of those first words uttered
A few of those awkward laughs mixed about a few awkward silences
Until it becomes a full on conversation and all either is saying is quiet
Because while one tells the other about what it is
They do during the day
The true communication lies between smiles
The other is pushing wider
Between eyes conveying all the words the mouth can't seem to make
In between these two people meeting right here, right now
For the first time
Ever

And they exchange what info they wish to disclose to each other
As life in this world of theirs must resume sometime
Lost in the panic, lost in the static, lost in the havoc
Found right here at the end of the earth

In love

Right here, right now

No one, including themselves, know how

No one knows how these things happen, but they do all the time

Any right here, any right now

These strangers have felt this sensation before, and
This is one of those sensations you don't choose to ignore

And these two lovers don't

Subsequently and sequentially
These moments happen

The first thing any young romantic needs to know
Is that hearts will be broken

The second is how to survive a broken heart

The third thing any young romantic needs to know
Is they will break a heart

The fourth is learning how

Jason Brain

THE DEEP WET CAFÉ KISS

The deep wet café kiss
sent a sensual orchestra
of music across the room,
dangling in conversation
sweet and delightful.

Her blonde windblown hair
shone radiantly amongst literary
photographs and vivid red brick.
Her dark haired counterpart
was shaded in debonair speech
revealing his unkempt presence.

They sat under an electric halo
of steaming coffee cups
while the young waiter determined
where he should go
to prevent being intrusive.

They held hands, fingers intertwined
when the operatic singer reached
crescendo through the speakers
reciting words of passion from deep
within the heart.

Their kiss grew in volume with each elevating note.
The hearth of love crackled in joyous divine.
A vibrant light wave zoomed back and forth.

They exited arm in arm

James Berkowitz

BETWEEN CREATIONS

The girls drop in like
exotic fruits
with their white dresses
chartreuse wraps and vined ribbons
with little beads of June moisture

They speak like breezes
eyes flickering
with light
lips pulsing with juicy messages
from the summer sky

The guys
like hulking crows
pick over
a table of nachos
not sensing the exotics yet

It's a moment of suspended forces
an intergalactic time between creations
before reflection
before
separation

Jack Cooper

WIDE WATER

A strange, somehow dangerous beatnik place —
some of the customers were barefoot — the waitress
with her long, straight hair was dressed in black.
The drinks were exotic — bitter espresso,
Constant Comment tea. We were 17.

Singers in rubber sandals pretended to be hillbillies —
since this was Boston, they sang of a "broken haht."
Then a woman sat at the mike with her guitar
and sang songs from Vanguard albums:

> *The water is wide, I cannot cross over*

and we held hands, poised at the edge of a bay.

> *And neither have I wings to fly*

We breathed her fingers' rhythm on the strings.

> *Give us a boat that will carry two*
> *And both shall row, my love and I*

Would anyone ever love me that much?
Why not us? Why not us, sitting in the smoky light
of a beatnik coffee house? Along the broad shore
the water would shine forever.

> *And both shall row, my love and I*

Lewis Gardner

THE WOMAN AT THE NEXT BOOTH
(Dupars Coffee Shop, 1992)

The woman at the booth
seated across from me
licks her upper lip
in a slow motion gesture —
sliding tongue against soft fleshy
skin.
With her right hand
she brushes a strand of hair
from her face.
For a moment I feel lost in
a phantasmagoric echo of fingers,
tongues, lips and hair all suspended
in slow moving motion.
The coffee shop is near empty
for an early Sunday morning
in the Valley off the 101 Freeway.
Our eyes meet briefly.
She quickly turns away.
I measure and record each feature,
eyes of of dark ebony, hair the shades of
burnt umber,
full bowed lips, the English aquiline nose,
the regal, the transcendent,
on a plane far above this earthy terrain.
In the restroom I argue with the mirror
on approaches and endeavors.
When I return a man slides into the booth
beside her.
Suddenly she has no motion,
no face.

JR Phillips

RESPONSE KU

I smelled the memory of your red hair and generous lips
Pressing their sweetness…having not met
I miss you…

Stephen Futral

THE THINGS I WOULD TELL YOU...
... IF WE EVER MET

We lay skin to skin - wrapped within each other
watching a movie, whose subtitles our eyes are too relaxed to read.
You ask me if she is pretty - "yes" I answer.
You drop a handful of names - "yes," I repeat,
"she's pretty. That one is beautiful. She is stunning."
Then you lay quiet - I lean into your thoughts.
Whisper - "the world is full of beautiful women - each desirable."
But it is you who I love - you my eyes see - wherever I turned.
"Would you make love to them all?" she says,
with a half-breath, that makes me think of Lauren Bacall.
"A sliver of me does. The me of my 20's does.
That me that drank women as if they where wine."
That was the greedy me.
The me that feared satisfaction and that reality
that I might be love-able.

I hold you - within the quiet between heart-beats -
I have no urge to run. Picturing you at 85 and I at 97.
Wrinkled and smiling we would still play that game of
'Is she pretty? Is she beautiful?' Saying 'no' would be a lie.
The only truth I know you need is my hand on yours,
my chest against your back, my lips upon your neck
and those three words you never tire of hearing.

Duane Kirby Jensen

GIRL INTERRUPTED

there's a girl inside
in a crocheted hat
twenty-five maybe
and pretty much all that
straight jeans and a cardy too
i'd talk to her now, if she were you

Trevor Maynard

IF YOU WERE MY GIRLFRIEND

If you were my girlfriend,
I would start my day
with an exultant spirit,
with the conviction
that I'm placed
in the sweetest realm ever,
a realm of your affection.

If you were my girlfriend,
I would comfortably slip through
Life's daily challenges
with the relief that there's someone
special, to share in my growing success.

If you were my girlfriend,
I would count my steps,
bear a permanent smile,
and cross every hurdle
with an ease, as though
it was only a simple test.

If you were my girlfriend,
I would aspire for greater heights,
swim on deeper oceans,
and walk through safer pathways,
to live in an air of satisfaction,
lingering a bit longer
to witness your ever lovely ways.

If you were my girlfriend,
I wouldn't feel a bit isolated
in being away from the outside world,
'cause in your presence, I'd find a companionship
far more lively than several encounters
in which I'd normally find alien.

If you were my girlfriend,
I would wish to conquer the world,
achieve the unachievable
and face the unrealizable.

But now you're my most special friend,
I would wish for nothing more
than to pray for an advancement
of our unavoidable attachment,
and wish... oh just wish

that you were my girlfriend!

Dowell Oba

FLASHBACK

We laughed over
grapefruit and vodka and promises
of great sex. And you asked
if I'd be your slave. But then
I am already.

And so, I'm giving up
for you. My Shakespeare sleeps
on my page and you lay
in my head where Hamlet hopes
to be – or not to be.

And now I recall your weight
in my arms. So pick the place
on the map of your body
that will tempt us
past reservation
and I will meet you there.

Scott Alixander Sonders

OF SWEETLY THEE I SOFTLY SING

In forming around and in you
I am realized anew
Derived once again
A borrowing from a northern tongue
In your southern hemisphere
Where I trace a line of saliva
In continents of sensation form and flux
I feel you shudder beneath me
Your moans the argot of ecstasy
The cant of delicious upheaval
I discover that which is my self
in every inch of you
Sculpted with the soft chisel of my lips

Were my sole work the invention of myself
In the expanding and contracting universe of you
My life and I would be thoroughly spent
In the arch and curve of the chambers of your heart

I have come home

Herbert T. Schmidt Jr.

A THOUSAND

"Michelle" – Painting by Carlos Scalise

Since you and I have ended
I've wept a thousand tears
Now I'm cold and alone
and I'm left with a thousand fears

The lights are on in this old house
however you've dimmed the lights to this old heart
It's warm and cozy within these walls
but I'm cold inside since we've been apart

When we were together
our love brought us a thousand smiles
Now I try to erase the memory of you
by riding my Harley a thousand miles

I've gone through a thousand bottles
to numb the pain that this heart break has brought
Losing the love that we shared
was harder to overcome than I ever thought

I look at a thousand pictures of us
so happy so wild and so incredibly free
All they are now are memories and reminders
of what will never be

We lit up a thousand nights
with fiery passion and burning ecstasy
Now I lay in bed cold and alone
without you next to me

Will we ever see each other again
or will we both live with a thousand regrets
Will we cash in this heartache for love
or live a lifetime with a thousand debts

Come back to me I miss you so much
Let's start all over and move ahead
I'm done living without you
One more tear I refuse to shed

I need you here, I need you now,
and I need you to be with me
Let's love each other for a thousand years
or better yet, for eternity

I love you Michelle

Carlos Scalise

TEARFULLY HOT

she had a sadness
in her eyes
that touched your soul

her shyness was pained
not a weakness
you understood
that she understood

her depths
showed an exquisite wisdom
an elegant shift of the mind
analyzing / cogitating
ultimately acting spontaneously
yet ever cautious

you know her heart
if you could only show her the confidence
to let go...to let her wild be
to chance the ecstasy again
though sadness may arise
you have to try
you have to partake / taste / jump in...

the joie de vivre
does not exist without the burning ice
of life's angst
the sadness of letting go
of attachment

you saw her wildness
just beneath the surface...guarded
if she melts she will turn to fire
and burn whomever gets close
to her heart

you ache for a taste
of her soul / her depths
her wild flames
igniting your flames

dancing barefoot
she was
tearfully hot

Stephen Futral

DUFFERIN.

So many knees in this new home. None like yours. Sores
on my eyes sussing a whole Ontario of shinbones.
You'd think the world was calf high, how I
demography it. But none measure remembering
the shush of your skirting past cubicle door, your
two lamb-landers glowing by.
Today I thought I saw you at St. Clair – legs
crossed. Blackened curl. I think I see you
everywhere and freeze like someone's walking
on your grave. Why I gave you
up to be "The Devil Dancing on the Pig-back
of the Globe" I'll never know.

Sean Cole

NOTHING QUITE LIKE

No other part of a woman's body
has the ability to express the undisciplined complexities
of her sexuality with anything near the completeness of her thigh

A woman's thigh is versatile
It is revealing and secretive
powerful and welcoming
and above all
honest

The thigh participates more thoroughly in the world
that swirls around a woman than
does any other part of her body

The thigh holds virtue as much for its own unique qualities
as for its proximity to other
anatomical delights

Fully clothed in jeans the line of the thigh holds a simple,
even innocent promise to it

Follow that line down and you are met
with the individual magic of the knee,
the calf and the ankle in rapid, enticing succession

Follow the thigh up and encounter the irresistible curve of the hip,
the fleshy, earthier comforts of the ass
and the ultimate cleft of desire

Half hidden by plaid, pleats or lace the thigh is a friendly tease
long on suggestions
but achingly short on definite answers

Fully revealed the thigh is a canvas to be painted with soft kisses,
gentle licks and even the occasional bite,
eliciting a furious swirl of color and heat

This is the picture brought forth by a happenstance glance of a
woman's thigh
climbing the stairs

stepping from a car
dancing with abandon
or casually stretched on the grass

A woman's thigh encompasses
both her strength and her vulnerability
her desire and her shadow self
her carelessness and her arrogance

and there is nothing
quite like

a
woman's
thigh

David McIntire

BETWEEN YOUR THIGHS

You appear again
Fixed in a forgotten pose
Fading into the pastels of nostalgia
Long after the fleet bird of youth has flown
From atop a stairway to the Venetian heaven
Your kingdom of my adoration
Between your thighs
Honeysuckle hyacinth lavender roux
The intoxicant the sweet fuel the elixir
Of the goddesses
Disguised briefly in denim cocked
At right angles to my hunger
Fecundity loaming in the beckoning wetness
Of Artemis the Santorinian heat of Hecate
In the presence of which I am struck mute
Robbed of thought stripped of conscience
In a time sans reason before age
When all was secret and all was shared
In that blonde summer of your divining

Herbert T. Schmidt Jr.

NO LAURA

Limb-splayed, all laconic, loose-lipped drunk
on lame impersonation, cockney game,
a double-Dutch-French-German-spouting dame,
not hapless frog nor hammering beast – but spunk,
hell, yes! Hell's bells! They toll for what I'd thunk
wrung hollow, harboring waves (no two the same)
of blurry prisons felled fast by a name
writ crimson smile: Petrarch's little punk

in spectacle, splayed on the billiard's felt
and cued for song, by honor, cheating trust
of ease. Bends her home/church/school/torso/rules
and throws fate: corner pocket, balling duels
at every turn, not Love's Elect but lust
wracked hard, not lingering long, her challenge dealt.

Scott Miller

AWAKENING

Amidst my slumber,
A sensation of soft lips,
On my shoulder blade,
Draw me from my dreams,
Into consciousness.

Eyes still closed,
My senses heightened,
By kisses delivered,
Like a butterfly.
To the nape of my neck,
To my cheek,
To my eyelids,
And settling on my lips.

Eyes open,
Responding to,
Your amorous call.
Warm arms wrap around,
Your warm body.
I wake from my dream,
Into another.

Andy Flatt

JACQUI

We toured amongst the Fauves.
I discussed her art in terms of mine.
She fed me meat and bread and oranges.

She verbally caressed the sanctity
of the human form until
I was ready to scream -- or worship.

She guessed eyes, but I confessed
it was her mouth I watched
when shapeless words ceased to satisfy.

I sipped my Jack Daniels
as slowly as possible, but
her Grand Marnier was forever emptied.

When she guessed at the time
she was an hour short --
I was more than two.

It is April already.
The days are getting longer.
God knows, I shouldn't look at her at all.

Rob Dakin

"Living with a whore--even the best whore in the world--isn't a bed of roses." — <u>Henry Miller</u>

MIRACLE WORKER

in a corner lot overgrown and murky,
shadowed with reality
a Mother works wonders

chicken hawk Love
face down in a nightmare
ignoring the smell of denial,
her talent was her gift

guilt was not an option
no longer to hear the tears of a torn soul,
she ran from the ropes to the street
to deliver more than her world could offer

at day's end, she counts the change
pennies to most, salvation to her
as the stench wraps her head, she drives
homeward to feed the one she would kill for

with tears steering her, she drives
the ruined reminder barely enough to carry her
a message of truth tattooed to the bumper

SUCK A DICK, SAVE A CHILD

Rob Dyer

HOOKERS ON ARCHER AVENUE

Late evening, early morning,
I search the night for whores,
young, bloody with desire.
Night streets are silent streets
except for hookers and their Johns.
One wants the dart of groins
the other green eyes in dollar
sacred treasures-
snatch the wallet, a consecrated craft.
Both hit the streets quickly
satisfy needs quickly.

I'm an old buck now rich with memories
more than movement, still talk, take porn shots,
with a peeking eye, snoop around
department store corners,
and dumpy old alleyways.
My hair is gray, my teeth eroding,
thoughts toward prayer
A.M. Catholic Mass,
then off in early morning
to the mailbox, a lethargic walk,
I pick up my social security check-
comforts my needs.

Evening settles into bed time
with a western romance novel,
ambushes, excitement,
old transgressions stretch
and relax.

No desires, homage
to the day, to the night.

Michael Lee Johnson

WHAT I DREW ON THE BAR NAPKIN

It was cruel that she was nude, for her and for me,
save for a mane so free-flowing,
her canvas habitat seemed a globe not given to gravity,
except where given to artistic license.

She was like Medusa
having spent the night slaying Perseus,
had trapped herself in the bathroom mirror the next morning.

At least the bartender liked it
liked it so much he hung her on a shelf,
pinched beneath a 12-year old bottle of scotch
liked it so much I got a short glass of bottom-shelf whiskey
for my trouble

she didn't seem to mind being put on display
there alone in a gallery of spirits, colors like stained glass
and only the fading spectre of her nostril-driven cigarette smoke
for company

I told the bartender about the last time I was in Las Vegas,
told him about a bible salesman named Mark
who bought me more liquor than I could drink

so long as I kept drawing him naked girls.
Mark told me he was trying to cheat on his wife,
I told Mark I could never remember the face of the first girl I loved

even when I was with her
so I drew a million pictures of the second girl,
so many she got sick of them,
so many that one day she finally suffocated
on her own caricature
lost in her hamburger helper,
Mark told me, they're all whores anyway.

I got up from my bar stool like the 1994 Northridge Earthquake,
took one more look at the girl dangling from the shelf
noticed, for the first time having staring at her all night

she didn't smile,
maybe because I brought her out of the ether
tethered her in ink forever to a 3-square-inch hygiene product

that would've otherwise been used to catch phone numbers
that would never be dialed.

The bartender told me to take it easy,
so I told him I couldn't take it any other way,
and as I left without tipping , I realized

in all the bars, on all the napkins hanging from shelves
or in apron pockets or shoved to the bottom of a purse or a trash bin
none of them had smiled, either tight or loose lipped

or mouth ajar like a perpetual exhale
or holding a cigarette between their inky lipstick smears
like it was a key they'd long forgotten what for

none of the girls smiled
and they never would.

Kris Huelgas

HOTT PANTS

the clothes you wear are screaming
those boots, yeah they really talk
there's a flair in the care of the wear of your hair
a sonnet when you walk
soft hint of hurt in the flirt of your shirt
a clitoral lean in your stand
haikus peek-a-boo through the hues of your rouge
wings sing from the ring on your hand
badass sunglasses made pretty good passes
but i read a whole book in that look
the doctoral thesis of fine little creases
i think there's a blink of mink in that wink
but that kink in your eyes
is the Nobel Prize

Steven Sassmann

BOW CHICKA WOW WOW

you turn me up
pretty lights
drown down on
all fours
dripping for more she
like we were never
supposed to meet
let alone fall in love
you dragged your
hair over me like hell
horses black on fire
joy rides the darkest hour
secret bright brutal
vicious piscis
twitter star
your uni verse
fast forward pause
happy childhood
goodbye shy
bible code matrices
zodiacs on my face
like a doll you
like a dominatrix
fear of evol my dear
the rules of love are
not contemplated here
complex diviner i am
primal anti climax
the how soon is now
she is the
bow chicka wow wow
a "V" form shining
a mouth of lights
strange flower like
red planet like
i might shed her skin
i might spread her wings
from me i stole
the heart of all
religions at your feet

you cast me out
my love unfurling
her toes curling
into themselves
discharged released
incompleted in you
put me down
keeping one finger
between my pages
centerfoldless

Vox Anon

FRECKLES

I love the way you jump when I smack your ass.
Seeing you standing in the kitchen at the stove
with your perfect butt; the look on your face as
you threaten me with the spatula is priceless.

I hate the way you push me away when you're angry,
slamming the door in my face, telling me to go fuck myself.
The hurt in your eyes is something I could never take.

I love how your hair smells in the evening when you
shake out your braid, the strands of long glistening brown
hair end up all over the place, the scent of shampoo
permeating the air as though you were fresh out of the shower.

I hate how you sound when you try to play stupid.
Knowing how smart you are it grates on my nerves when
you act like you don't know something.
I hate fact that you don't know that infuriates me.

Watching you sleep at night is probably the single most
beautiful thing I have seen in a long time.
I've counted the freckles on your face at least one hundred
times while listening to you snore softly. Yes. You do snore.

Seeing you talk to your bitchy friends is almost revolting at times.
How can you be friends with women, who as far as I can tell,
have absolutely no redeeming qualities whatsoever?
You need better friends.

The way you look at me when you're horny drives me insane.
Even in the middle of a crowd I can tell by the way your eyes
sparkle, and that little lift of your right eyebrow.
You have me wrapped around your finger, don't you?

Some of the things you say are just so painful, even though
I know you don't mean them.
I'm not prepared to fight back; I know that's what you want.
I'm just not programmed that way. I wish I could heal your scars.

Your past still haunts you. Your past haunts me too.
My past was empty. My future with you is what matters to me.
You're scared of the future; always worried. Looking at your past
I can't blame you for feeling that way.

I wish I could help you passed your past.
I know our future is bright once that happens.

I'm starting to see changes in you;
the strength of your smile has grown.
You've stopped hanging out with your old friends.
You don't even flinch anymore when I wrap my arms around you
from behind. I wish I knew how you got past it, but I don't care.

I love every piece of you, especially all 189 freckles
on your beautiful face.

Troy Pickens

THE GIRLS ON STAGE

I'm a red-blooded man, I'll freely admit!
I've spent lots of time in rooms dimly lit.
Topless women, drinks, and lap dances;
Funny, how those things make men feel like princes.

Idiotic, and sad, but oh, it's so true!
Bared breasts and T-back and yeah, the tattoo;
Drinks flowing freely at ten bucks a pop.
Reach out with a hand and catch that lace top.

Intoxicating and exciting, it is!
You almost detest the need to go piss.
Knowing you'll miss the most glorious sets;
Double D's, or C's; whatever she gets.

But then comes a time it's no longer fun;
Many dollars spent, and no prizes won.
It takes many years to slowly sink in:
These women are ladies, not honors to win!

Too many are friends now, some of my best.
I do hope they'll take some time for a rest.
But, the money is good and men are such fools;
They spend and they spend with hope for their Tools.

So, now I've stepped back, no longer a youth,
With memories of women, some think uncouth.
I love them all, be they short, blonde, or tall;
Those marvelous women paid to bare all!

Steven Gadberry

196

THE GIRLS

the girls aren't real,

slender-finger spider-women,
canvas girls, in tone and wardrobe,
ballerinas, en pointe, unscrewed from music boxes,
expanded, clothed
in electric tether and blues
sewn from vibrating needle points

they are the Mexican girls with red lipstick
with names like Virginia or Marilyn

They play the guitar, or the bass, or the piano,
or all of them, and just as good as their ex-boyfriends
let alone, girlfriends,
and they've read twice the books you have

here are facts,
these are the girls that exist not in tangible space,
flat ground,
but in the ether,
with by-chance vibrations visible in our spectrum.
in the mouths of the skinny-talls, in the world of no mimesis,
tattooed-bearded guys
riding bicycles
made of MFAs and dreams

Kris Huelgas

LISA AND DALI AND ME

she flaunts her vices
and tries too hard, to be
different.

sees herself a poet
-truth is, she is dreadfully
mediocre. nevertheless,
she is a friend.

thinks she has to be dark and mysterious
and miserable;
when she gets bored,
she has sex
with men who
don't love her,
strangers
and sometimes
women,

just to be…different.

tonight we sit in the dark
in her family's guest house
just off Mulholland,
getting drunk.
she talks of how she despises
her parents
affluence- again.

all the while,
her store bought L.A. body
is draped in
Versace
and the keys to her
Porsche
rest comfortably
in the six hundred dollar
Fendi cocktail purse,
she's tossed on the floor.

I open another beer,
as she snorts another line
off of the signed
Dali lithograph she
had me remove from the wall.
it's not the good Dali,
it's the later, pedestrian, diluted Dali;
you know,
the stuff he churned out
just for the money towards the end.

(kind of fitting really)

I snicker at the way they're
so proud of it, yet appropriately,
even if by accident,
it hangs at the end of the hall.

ten minutes ago
she asked if I wanted a
blow job,
I wonder what this says
about my company.

I may take her up on her offer though,
I'm feeling
a bit disillusioned
myself.

Kevin Craig

THE ACTRESS

All this fame,
still a million men
walk down the road
without knowing you.

You tell me this over a tall glass.

I recognized you
but did not let you know.
The actress in you walked
a few paces behind you,
a tall shadow
between the manicured complexes,
plazas and the cafés in a foreign make up.

You tell me over a tall glass- you have a famous name.

I look at the actress
waiting outside,
lengthening by the falling day,
its eyes darkening.
I know her.
But I can walk on a road
without acknowledging this.

Kushal Poddar

LILLY, LONELY TRAILER PROSTITUTE

Paint your face with cosmetic smiles.
Toss your breast around with synthetic plastic.
Don't leak single secrets to strangers-
locked in your trailer 8 foot wide by 50 foot
with twisted carrots, cucumbers, weak batteries,
and colorful dildos-you've even give them names:
Adams's pleasure skin, big Ben on the raise, Rasputin:
the Mad Monk-oh no, no, no.
Your legs hang with the signed signatures
of playboys and drifters ink.
The lot rent went up again this year.
Paint your face with cosmetic smiles.

Michael Lee Johnson

CUT

We met at a Halloween party. She came dressed as a man and I was looking for a father figure. Costumed in a monk's habit borrowed to cloak my hippie stench and lend a purpose to my ragged beard. Her blue eyes were mostly unconvinced and old beyond her years.

The accent spoke a history: Texas shrimp boat trash, a junior high drop-out with a hitch in her grammar: *I done gone* to Beauty College where she learned to cut hair at 15 and married already to a big soft daddy man come home every night hold her in his lap and she would cry cry cry without even knowing why.

It was all wrong that trailer park — the country music, the missing spark. Moved to Houston with the boom money gushing and all them heads and her like a machine — hour after hour — like an International Harvester she would cut that hair.

The people they talked how every cut framed perfectly the particulars of that face — no matter the shape or what unnamed hell played behind the eyes — the after was better than the before.

Galveston she drove us that first night. Scissors flashed in wet moon light. Leaned, her breath in my ear, *I want to cut you*. There in the dark, cross-legged on the beach, She cut by feel, her fingers reached, dug like vermin into my scalp while the waves beat blue spume and severed hair fell across my back.

A wedge-cut it was called. A short style popular among women at the time. With a touch of eye-liner, I too looked much better after than I had before.

Good enough to step into her house of no doors.

No bedroom door.
No bathroom door.
No place to hide.

Mornings I made her Luzianne coffee dripped in a blue enamel pot, sweetened with Eagle Brand condensed milk spooned from the can.

"Make it sweeter," was her command.

Then off to the salon, hair still wet, skin reeking of rose oil and ambition, cut fourteen heads and buy me a new dress. Back home I'd fix some dinner, massage her neck. She'd fuck me from behind and leave me to the mess. Arrange herself on the floor, kimono snugged against her breasts, she'd throw the I Ching and read out loud, full-throated like hungry bird, from the Book of Changes.

Mel Green

ST PETERSBURG

On the frozen square
The black spikes of the trees
Thrust spears into the sky.

The cone of the cathedral spire
Is a fist, thrust
Defiantly into the fundament of God.

This morning's snow
Now cleared away
Black boots still tread carefully.

Anna Nikolaevna
Why is your skirt
So short?

Are two pairs of black stockings
Enough
To keep out the cold?

Your porcelain breasts
Rub your blouse naked
In your short black coat.

You pause by the chestnut seller
Inhaling the rich roast scent
But you have no money to buy.

These high grey concrete slabs
That you share with ten thousand souls
Squat solid mausoleums.

The elevator as usual is broken
Six stories your sharp heels clip behind
In the dismal grey tunnel of stairs.

Your eyes of pale blue Slavic sky
Hard and kind and full of lies
Drop as you fumble for the key.

Anna Nikolaevna
You fold your blouse and skirt
So neatly.

Your red tongue
Flickers against your narrow lips
Sharp as an asps.

Avoid the broken bedspring
The mattress slumps
Under your square full hips.

The sky through the window
Bare of clouds
Black arrowheads swoop,

And their wings
Take the seriousness from your eyes
With them into the sky.

Thomas Kent

CROWBAR KISSES

there is a suction in the touch, the reach, the rush
whichever of the two of us would dare come out first…
questions asked elapse unaccountably passed
through the tell-tale heart...
law of kings, rule of thieves,
the wild call of the kettledrum beats
with sideward glances and crowbar kisses.

seemingly here where I know nothing
of these lives in my sight….
like a burglar i break into your sea of change;
left with nothing to do but to be here with you.
time, love, life – things meant to be answers -
somewhere in the everything of each of us,
i see with an eye that is one in the storm of such…
where the depth of the primeval forest dark
is seductive, inspired and created by some mad god
at play in the machinery of life...
 law of kings , rule of thieves,
the wild call of the kettledrum beats
with sideward glances and crowbar kisses.

GROWL of morning, the city yawning,
truth is I have no idea how to emerge with trust;
then I see her smile in storm of rage,
clash and chase for green-paper-power-gold.
in these streets i drop from exhaustion,
clumsy as an exposed lie…
down to the bottom
the dead raise history to an art.
from inside the wind she is reborn
with wings for feet.

i do not know the sparrow's soul
or have i walked the lion's realm
i only know the poet and the con man
both of whom i know so (very) well
i cannot help myself i give in to the flesh
so much treasure to uncover
to tempt, to trespass or to test...

law of kings, rule of thieves,
the wild call of the kettledrum beats
with sideward glances and crowbar kisses.

Joey Alkes

"The death of a beautiful woman is, unquestionably, the most poetical topic in the world." — <u>Edgar Allan Poe</u>

EXORDIUM
for my third-grade teacher

she wore
her hair
in one long braid,
wound around
the top of her head
until it became
an alabaster pillbox –
prim standard
of her unwavering
propriety.

she was neither
oblivious to
its effect
upon her pupils
nor deterred by
our unruly gibes –
in the end,
the pillbox prevailed
(so it continued
through april --
we flouted
every primer,
learning nothing).

six a.m.
one bright may morning,
early to school,
i padded mischievously
down the asbestos corridor
to peer in
at her classroom door;
puckish surprise
my puerile aim.

inside,
she sat –
a septuagenarian sylph
serenely brushing

six feet of
undulating alban
gossamer.

i remember
weightlessness,
reverie,
light
and music;
nothing in
nine years
on earth
had prepared me
for such
ineffable
radiance.

i stood
transfixed;
one glorious moment
in Dian's presence
before backing away
with shame
hissing
in every cilia.

later,
her immaculate cataract
restored to
pristine cylindrical obeisance,
she expounded upon
the virtues of cursive
and made perfect
chalk spirals
to inspire
fit chirography.

having *seen* her,
i scribbled stupidly
and dreamt of
wings ...

                                        Rich Follett

BARE YOUR NAKED SOUL

She possess a natural beauty
That all must see to believe
When I look into her soul baring eyes
I see the distance in between

The magical world that she resides
Tantalises the child in everyone
I look at her but I dare not stare
For it's like looking into the sun

She moves with such grace and style
That she's carried upon a cloud
She's the one for most famously
Standing out amongst the crowd

She bares her naked soul
For all of us to see
Addressing our emotions
In my mind she's undressing me

In an out-of-body-experience
A naked soul in ritual dance
The lady in the spotlight
Enters a mystical trance….

She's captured our minds
and won our hearts
The only thing left to give is our lives
and here… I'll make a start.

I offer myself as a sacrifice
On the altar of pure love
My pure naked soul takes flight
On pure white wings of a dove
I join the lady in the light
And stare into the sun
Now I can look into her eyes
For our souls are now one

Mick Jones

POT-POURRI OF A MOTHER'S MIND

pot-pourri of mother's mind,
dipped into the melancholy soup,
thoughts about her children,
heart wandering for her husband's face

toys of her child
rusting around the house,
photos of her husband
resting on the bed

amassing all the picture of years,
she today cooks with her tears,
in soup of love,
she shelves her salt
to prepare a dish
in memories of
loving relations she had once...

Pawan Hira

MY MOTHER'S SALT

1.
My mother cooked with salt,
flavoring our lives
with the spice of her choice . . .
A white grain from the sea
that added new worlds of taste
to children made of mixed spices.
2.
My father loved his pepper
heating up her pot
with its red flames,
that little masculine bulb
men use to show bravado
about nothing.
3.
We ate of Mother's salt
all of our lives till we grew
old enough to insist
she travel to the sea
of her spice, away from the red heat
of our father's pepper.
4.
Today, fifteen years on
my mother has stopped
cooking with that spice
as white as my father's skin.
And we have grown accustomed
to his hot spice,
hardly remembering
her love for little white grains
drawn from the sea.

Nicholas Damion Alexander

GRANDMA CHAIN SMOKING

Lighting one cigarette off the butt of another 4:00AM.
Radio humming low just for company, a human voice in the room.
Did your thoughts keep you awake?
The losses of a lifetime impossible to recoup or calibrate.
Feelings with immeasurable weight pressed down on your chest.
Hard to breathe in a vacuum of memories all strung on a clothesline,
Flapping in the wind.
Grandma, I now comprehend so much of your lonely struggle.
Why some of us must sit wide awake at 4:00AM.
Wrestling with words to make light of the pain.
A prayer uttered in silence.
A station dutifully kept.
A heart to heavy to sleep.

Kevin M. Hibshman

SOFTLY & LOUDLY SHE CRIES (17/30)

"Illness is not a metaphor." – Susan Sontag

against the brutal ellipses
the cruel punctuation of her days
the shortness of breathing room
the illimitable poverty of pain
that wraps like a chain
anchors her to the couch
squeezing time from her skin
solar flares from her blood
and inevitability from her wanton joy

there is no mystery here
just a woman alone with her pain

David McIntire

GRAVEL ROAD

she brings a bowl
of ripe apricots
to this lonely room
where my body rots from within

for a while the walls fall away
I breathe without the burn, the choke

she removes the flesh
with just her bare hands
until left with only the hard pit
which she smashes with a hammer
extracts and feeds me the seeds
with some small chunks of ice

she wears a yellow dress
redolent of southern summers
returning from my youth
over nothing but her skin

she is what the sunlight
through the pale blue curtain
strains and fails to be

I search her eyes,
find a reason to believe
when she says,
"the tumors are dying not you"

then her smile breaks soft and clean
touches everything at once
just enough to get inside
now I can sleep.

William Crawford

QUIET HOURS PASSING

You rest
in this empty hospital room.

Your repetitious words, spoken to yourself,
stumble over one another.
Everything is in holes and pieces.

The strange ear-ringing sounds of silence
broken by occasional voices in the hall-

the shadows pushing the lights
around like street bullies-

the sparse furniture all changed,
each strange piece placed differently than
you would have it at home.

But you're not at home, you're
in this empty hospital room, resting.
Everything is in holes and pieces.

Michael Lee Johnson

THE VICTIM'S RED DARKNESS

The victims' unit
has a larger than Alice window.
Its curtains bandage the world.
The nurse collecting the samples
from the victim's
under-nails and between-legs spaces
proclaims-
the windows are sealed
and no suicide is allowed.
The magic potion on the table,
a transparent spider hangs from one clean corner,
red patches waltzes on the curtains.
The victim watches
the window shrinks;
the day corrodes and memory returns
bleeding down the detours.
Ten convex nails grow from her under-nails.
They want to scratch off her between-legs dark patch.

Kushal Poddar

KITCHEN WINDOW

She stands and does not see me.
Stock-still as if dreaming awake.
I sense a lifetime of unresolved questions
hovering just above my own.
Is it pain that truly shapes a beautiful soul?

She stares out a weary window, sentinel at her post.
I cannot fathom her silent vision.
I wonder what is out there to be seen?
Perhaps I am a child again
and my mother is gazing at a world
we all must surrender?

Kevin M. Hibshman

PLEASE

You were looking at the moon,
or perhaps you were bored.
Nevertheless, the window owned your eyes
as you stared.
And there and then
a wide streak, a pale imprint
or glow washed over you in a kind of regal holiness,
revealing the landscape of your freckled flesh,
your skin a place for the softest kisses,
mane of hair mid-spine,
woven it seemed out of sweet summer grass.
I remember.

There is not a natural rescue in this drama,
no reason on earth why you should forgive me,
yet I'll lift my face and ask anyway:
Please?

Len Kuntz

HINGE
for Ginny

Dirt sweeps the sweet earth
with a loamy promise of growth,
holding the grass just tight enough
to let each blade sway

in its own green way. Water carries
flotillas full of tourists and sunscreen,
all-you-can-eat buffets buffeted
by a glittering surface which serves

as invitation to drown, and buoy
against the ocean's dark end.
Breath is taken for granted.
Flames lick the air, banish the cold

and our daughter holds us
like a hinge. We pivot around her
because that's our design. Without her
we'd be a simple wooden door, latched shut.

Robert Wynne

HOUSE FOR SALE

The windows were still
curtained in fine lace,
as on the day she changed them
pending her hoped-for return.

I approached the rear door,
half expecting mother's smile
greeting my day-long
homecoming from school.

No care-worn face
peered in apprehension at
the sound of footfalls broaching
this most intimate way in.

No television screen flickered
by the gas-misering fire;
all was closed, hard-closed
and bolted from within.

Only my own reflection
returned my stealing gaze
through the leaded window
where evenings she would sit

nursing fading memories
where fresh flowers grow,
acknowledging a half-known face
appeared above the hedge.

I twist the key in grudging lock,
stooping to gather the clutter
of uncorresponding mail
on my tentative way in;
pausing by half-open door
of the denuded living-room,
its empty hearth in fire-roaring,
family-assembling afterglow

down the deserted years

that bind the long-dead
with those whose voices rang
until barely hours ago.

David Mallinson

"...it was her habit to build up laughter out of inadequate materials." — John Steinbeck, *The Grapes of Wrath*

MOTH LIGHT
for Grace Paynter

the lines
on her face
tell you
laughter
wasn't always
a stranger here

William Crawford

MY SWEET

I've been instructed otherwise,
yet I often think of the girl you were before —
buried in bubble baths,
favoring foot lotions and
lilac-scented cashmere,
bursting out in song or
giddy laughter that could shake a room.

Now fluff from the afghan collects like diaphanous peach fuzz
around your chin, one feather
latched in the deepest crease of a cheek,
laugh line put there from your steady smiling,
before the stroke,
before all of the dead-end silence

But when I move to wipe away a dribble of spittle,
your eyes hitch with a diamond glimmer
before flattening out again
and I know what you've done,
that you've just smiled at me,
saying, I'm here,
saying, My Sweet. Don't forget us, My Sweet.

Len Kuntz

M IS FOR MOTHER

She sits quietly, staring diligently at the television,
as she watches Shelley slap Paul for sleeping with Deidre,
or smiling when Ken blackmails Joyce after he discovers
the DNA test results that prove that Samuel is Raven's real father. She
watches this serial every day, every day, whether the leaves outside
are turning plum or tangerine, or if the snow cascades off bristling
tree branches.

Every morning she has half a cantaloupe with a small yogurt,
coffee black, as she sits on the bar stool by the kitchen counter,
taking small deliberate bites, always leaving about one third
of the fruit uneaten. She sits in darkness, whether it is sunny
outside, or whether the moon hangs gingerly in the midnight sky.
Such is her world.

At nine-thirty every night, she settles into bed, listening
to Mike Huckabee, or an old rerun of The Virginian
on the television, or she calls her friend Helen
to check in, say goodnight, before repeating the same routine
again tomorrow, finding comfort in these rituals.

Occasionally, she will go with Duane to the grocery store
as he hustles to grab two percent milk and tv dinners
to place into the cart. He will then drive her home, laughing
at her witty observations, how people talk to their pets
as if they were children or how children outfool
slick, strict parents. She is always spot on, even if she cannot
actually see.

Sometimes she will sit in silence listening to the whir
of the washing machine, or to the clink, clink, clink
of the ice maker, waiting until 5 p.m., when her neighbor
Susie will come to rap on her door bellowing,
"Where's my drink?", to which she will reply,
"I thought you'd never come." They will laugh and talk
about emerging taxes, the state of the nation's economy,
how her husband left her far too soon, or how her friends,
one by one, are passing on, leaving her to face the new day
alone, or how grateful she is for having watched
the world change in the past century, or how lucky

she is to have the love of her granddaughters who call twice
a week, making her laugh and smile.

She sees, but she doesn't see, and somehow, in some way,
she accepts what is, and does not question why not, nor make any
allowance to feel sorry for herself. She can accept this because the
world is going to change anyway, and all she can do is hang on for
the ride. Just hold on. Just hold on tight. All she can do is hold on.

Michael Wayne Holland

I KNEW
for my maternal grandmother Helen Stewart Whitehouse

i knew
even as i ascended the stairs,
carrying her dinner on a filigree tray:
it was over.

fifteen is so young to know
but i did know –

and so did she.
her life was measured in giving;
so much
for so long
to so many
that we
who received her
selfless abundance
had long since abandoned
outward shows of gratitude

(we were not above thanks; rather,
she was embarrassed by
the merest morsel of appreciation) –

she existed solely to give;
we learned that accepting
was the kindest recompense.

she gave us sundays
around an ancient multifoliate mahogany table

on creaking, faux medieval
red-seated crackled pigskin chairs
(grandfather's was the only one with arms);
she gave us food beyond imagining –
perpetually overcooked;
each course gray and lifeless
yet somehow ambrosial –
served between snippets of
minced Methodist hymn

(grandmother could neither cook nor sing
but paid no heed to destiny
in pursuing her passions).
she gave us a place at the table –
a place to rise above our shared DNA.

she gave us
ourselves.

it was because she had given so much
that i knew
it was over
when she asked me to feed her.

one paper-thin, velvet touch of her furrowed hand
on my anguished cheek
heralded her obsequy:

'Lambie, would you…?'
Lambie would;

Lambie did;

knowing full well
what it meant –
what it took for her to ask.

an elegy in applesauce;
one teaspoon, just level –
tissue-thin lips on generations-old silver,
a glimmer of rheumy, empathic understanding;
a flicker behind the cataracts
and then

for one terrible, beautiful moment
i glimpsed the universe of pain
from which her infinite gifts had sprung.

a delicate, labored swallow;
the rustle of lilac curls on crisp linen;

i remember

(or perhaps only wished for)
her featherlight kiss on my fretful brow
as i leaned in to say goodnight.

i knew
even as i descended the stairs,
carrying her dinner on a filigree tray:

it was over.

fifteen is so young to know
but i did know –

and so did she.

Rich Follett

DESERVES

this was my love, mine own true love
who lies waiting to go underground
in life a red rose, and now so pale
Irish brandy to water transformed
jalapeña caliente turned ice
aiee! And now the people close 'round
some loved her, some knew her
and some knew only her tongue
ah! ah! the blackrobe walks in
soon he'll stand and tell us his lies
and who knew her, who loved her will weep
to hear her life so betrayed
if this were the service that she deserves
a coyote would stand by her bier
an owl would sit at her feet
and no one would speak
but a raincloud would prowl
and the earth would rumble and shake
and when night would fall
the roof would pull back
and we'd stare at a night full of stars
at the peak of the dome one would brighten its light
til our eyes hardly could watch
then slowly it'd dim til it winked out at last
and the owl would spiraling climb
til we couldn't see it, maybe from dark
the coyote would cough and dissolve
and we'd slip away, one or two at a time
and her body would vanish in flame

Wyatt Underwood

NEVER SIT WITH YOUR MOTHER AT A FUNERAL

In the slightest movement of a trembling hand
my mother slid the watch around her wrist
so that she could glance down at it without
other mourners noticing her impulse.
Not that she was disrespecting the dead,
but I guess there's only so much pain a
classically trained musician can endure.
Do you hear that rumbling noise? she whispered,
nodding at the speaker of the tiny organ
wreaking havoc on "Sheep may safely graze."
It's the sound of Bach turning in his grave.
A moment's silence fell between us, then
suddenly overcome, we bowed our heads,
shoulders shaking, while sympathetic friends
gave us tissues to wipe away the tears.

Andrew Kreider

ALUM, LIME AND TIME
for Patti Thisted Arthur

two pickles in a mason jar --
Shenandoah dill,
grass-green and crisp;
wrinkled viridian jewels
inveigling clear through
the closed door
of the refrigerator.

no side dishes, these;
rather, transcendent
bonnes bouches of brine --
each a petite paean
to halcyon summer.

one week ago,
the jar was full --
gift from a friend's kitchen;
the work of her loving hands.

in the time since,
my wife and i
(with childish grins
and dripping chins)
have savored each one so fully
as to have numbered and named them
with our delight;
thanks-praying for these benisons
(as dear to us as fleeting youth) and
repenting our reckless pickle lust
even as we reached
with giggling, guilty fingers
for another …

one week ago,
the jar was full;
one week ago
the vibrant,
extraordinary young woman who
blessed us with

sunshine from a crock
was at our door --
today,
news of her passing.
incomprehensible, really,
that two pickles
in a mason jar
could be
all that remains --
the only tangible remnant
of her sweetness
in our life;
it is
so inexpressibly cruel
for the line between
here and gone
to be so fine,
the parting
so sudden.

here in our kitchen,
i stand in my bathrobe
feeling a chill
clear through
the closed door
of the refrigerator.

one week ago,
i would not have believed:
tonight
i open the refrigerator door
just to stare at
two pickles
in a mason jar
(two perfect, beryl lobes);
open the door,
hold my breath
and pray --
hoping against hope
that i will see them begin
to beat.

Rich Follett

REQUIEM

a friend's funeral happened
a thousand miles away
a dozen people held umbrellas
rain fell desultorily
a man who meant well
spoke of a life he hadn't known
I wonder what I would have said
we'd not been close nearly ten years
she loved life when I knew her
rode horses and climbed rock
sat on a cliff's edge and laughed
until I grimaced and joined her
trees I knew grew fifty feet tall at least
looked like dollhouse toys
"I'd take the fast way down"
she laughed, "if I could make the stop soft"
she grinned at me
"I couldn't stand to miss tomorrow,
what all might happen?"
but last week she put a gun into her mouth
and blew the pain away, so close friends say
I hope her way made the stop soft

Wyatt Underwood

AND A NORMAL DAY IT WAS

And a normal day it was,
I still remember,
my mom running errands of the day,
readying me for the school
finding the hidden tie somewhere in
the old cottage

and I had a last look then,
she was up in the early morning
we broke no words,
but she found my tie and left
for the backyard.

a secret died with her
following her suicidal act,
for a year she was on her deathbed
heart beat consorting, but no motion,

in a coma she was for life…

and what was the reason ?
Was it my parent's materialistic values
or their reflection of love for their daughter
to marry her off at an early age
to save her from evil eyes of society -
what was it?
In days, she was heading for a new life,
coloured with new family,
to wed a puppet of my parent's eye

still at this young age,
I could try to reason myself,
what was in her heart?
Did she know something strange about her
future life?
Was there no hope left in her?
And did she not think about alternatives

before hanging herself with the cruel rope
around the death fan?

Was her heart was so weak,
that it could not burst out with true feelings?

and how did she find a rope?
With sun shining,
how did the thought of ending life
come into her psyche
wish I could knew then,
wish I could sense something
and wish my parents were not thinking
about the good future of her…

Pawan Hira

LIFTS HER LIKE A CHALICE

The weekday Mass at 6 a.m.
brings the old folks out
from bungalows
around the church.
They move like caterpillars
down sidewalks,
some with canes,
some on walkers.

Father Doyle says the Mass
and then goes back to the rectory
to care for his mother
who cannot move or speak
because of a stroke.

And every Sunday at noon
when the church is full,
Father Doyle, in full vestments,
wheels his mother
in a lump
down the middle aisle
and lifts her like a chalice
and places her in the front pew
before he ascends to the altar.

Sometimes at night,
when his mother's asleep,
Father Doyle comes back to the Church
and rehearses in the dark
three hymns she long ago
asked him to sing at her funeral.

He practices the hymns
because the doctor said
she could go at any time.
When that time comes,
he doesn't want to miss a note.
The last thing she ever said was
"Son, I'll be listening."

Donal Mahoney

MOTHER

Mother.
It wasn't in the poverty
Of having to burn your shoes
To keep your children warm -
Nor in damp walls – or
Peeling wallpaper.

It wasn't in the cutting-cutting
Draft through cracked windows –
Under warped doors -
The hunger pains
Or red runny noses.

It was witnessing your
River of sad silent tears
As you tried to protect me
In that moment our eyes
Met – in a before language -
Look.

It's the desperate aching
That poverty feeds:
When you starve yourself
For others
Cutting slices of bread
Thin enough for seven.

You thought you gave us
Nothing - when you gave us everything:
Love.

Nursery rhymes from heart -
Shown us another world in
Misty drawings
Across cracked window panes.

Two hours before you died
Aged eighty two – much reduced -
Lying there so very small -
I whispered to you:

"The Owl and the Pussy Cat went-
To Sea in a beautiful....."

And a single tear – a
Single tear - tracked down your
Cheek. A last tear
That I kissed away.

Roger Cornish

AND A PILGRIMAGE WAS WRITTEN FOR HER

and a pilgrimage was written for her,
with prayer beads in her sacred hands

on a ritual of meditation every hour in the morning; that day
she multiplied the time for long enough
that I had to disturb her shoulders,
to ask for the petit déjeuner
Such radiance in her ageing eyes could I see
that it bunkered within me
for hours

it was late evening then –
only to see
a diametrical sky, shaded with nimbuses,
plucking the acrid leaves of verandah, I
dared to look at her.
she was ready to leave
for ten days of bliss
but barren fields of her face,
caught in a drought
pale skin stretched, leaving impressions of bleakness,
the morning charm was withering with dusk
and my father couldn't even level with her eyes,
he berated her instead,
devising parody of her life.

She took the bus,
without even looking back
and a moment of dying silence came forth –
if her voice stops,
would my father sob in her virtuous clothes?

Pawan Hira

SEVERED ON APRIL FOOL'S DAY

In loving memory of Martita Aldea Casey Hanson, my mother.

I remember when my mother died,
the first of April a decade ago.
Standing at the foot of her hospital bed,
looking down upon her frail form
I watched her final breath evanesce.

The circle of flesh around her pallet
composed of her children, all holding hands
winced in sudden pain, simultaneously,
the rush of grief exploding within us.
A stupefying chill lanced my midsection.

My logical, prefrontal cortex,
the rational heart of my mind
tells me it was the start of catharsis,
the expected emotional realization
that a sentimental connection had ended.

But my reptilian brain knows otherwise
and with a comprehension beyond common
perception, it felt what I now know to be true,
an invisible umbilicus had
been severed between my mother and me.

The sensory recoil of this spectral
surgery rocked me back upon my feet.
My sister-in-law steadied me with her arms.
I burst into tears and shook uncontrollably,
shocked by these alien, afferent assaults.

There are mysteries beyond comprehension,
and wiser men than I duel daily as
swords of science contend with rapiers of religion.
Yet beyond this ageless battleground
I have experienced an eternal truth.

The inexplicable and unseen tether
of love between a mother and her child.

Michael H. Hanson

AUNT GLADYS
(died of influenza, aged 22)

Her life as it might have been
lies here in this unwritten book
releasing virgin pages
to the messengers of time;
recording only sketches for
a life from chance remarks
of those who knew her well
and cherished in her echoed prime.

'How graceful, how like a flower
she hung upon her father's arm.'

This, and sundry details
culled from lives sprung up
and thrived around her, tell
of where she lived, and how,
and in what time her beauty
yielded to the rare-ripe scythe.

David Mallinson

AUNT BETTY

you say, "It's great you could make it kid,
it means a lot to me, it really does,"
reaching up to me then. I know,
with your open arms...
Unable to be there at your beside Aunt Betty
because I'm not being told
when I don't even know
that your health has turned bad
I can only speak
saying psyches iatreion
from this later date, when your soul
is following some course
surmised correctly, or not
finding a loop under a lightning storm
my dad ready to offer us his ice breaking humor
hiding his worry of the moving sky.
unable to be there at your bedside,
because I'm not being told,
when I don't even know, but hear
your comprehending, investigating
"Stay where you are," you say
speaking to me about the most recent
people that I live among, and your discovery
which happens quickly within a few lines
of my voice, of everything that's going
on with me, not a stone left unspoken to
of my life at the moment,
your request of me to sing in poetry
the pond, Johnny and I coming
running into the house covered in mud
you giggling, you still giggling,
has kept me laughing my
entire life, but you, that story
about my Uncle saying, "I'll take care of
this," picking up Johnny and me,
and putting us both under the shower
fully clothed, I don't know what
from my mother followed but I
know I followed Johnny around

the house, before we wound up,
psyche iatreion,
in our library together with you

Albert George Geiser

AUNT CILE

She was the smile
that gilded Texas wheat stalks
my first summer in this country.
She was the breeze
that cooled the Baptist hellfire
each Sunday morning that first year.
A thousand stories
wove a hammock to the plains
a frightened stranger could rest in
safe from the wind
that drove his unstrung balloon
far to the south, to his old home.
She raised the moon
bright on panhandle wheat waves
as its bridge on Brazilian breakers.
Stays as moon's smile
stretches to a belly laugh,
grins down to a memory of light.

Wyatt Underwood

DOGWOOD DAYS

Seattle Dogwood © Apryl Skies

She sits in glistening darkness
most of the time, as bitter blood flows
through fragile veins, pulsing, hearing
the beat of her heart, the beat of robust rain,
a beat that alludes defeat, and I always make certain
that across the room she has flowers smiling
brightly at her. Yellow daffodils are her favorite,
and out of a pale pinhole, she can see,
just barely see, see the crystal vase full
of something so exquisite, it warms her,
soothes her, brings buoyant joy
in a pure package, just for her.

She never complains of limitations. Instead,
she talks about the dogwood tree
that grew in the yard where she lived
on a farm as a young girl, how majestic and full
of life it possessed, so vital, unabashedly unafraid,
just growing and feeding its rich soil.
Or she speaks of the magnolia that only displayed
three buds the year my father passed,
and how the very next year, the branches
were full with blossoms, or how in late summer,
she could smell and taste the honeysuckle

hailing from the open field just across the street
from the first house she lived in after marrying
my father, and how the rosemary grew wild
as she would pluck it and use in her baked chicken.

She sees out of that tiny, tiny precious pinhole,
but all she sees is something vivid, something
beautiful, and tells stories, stories most people
take for granted, stories that should be told
to grandchildren, stories that should be passed
on from generation to generation, stories
some people will embellish, or some people
forget, stories that quiet and comfort
my soul, and make me appreciate her: my mom,
her challenges, how she views beauty, just sees beauty,
just beauty, and comprehends, and never complains,
or feels pity for herself. That is the true gift
she taught me, one that I do not forget,
one that I know, love, one that leaves
me breathtakingly speechless.

Michael Wayne Holland

HOW THINGS HAPPEN

Charlotte is dead; black lab, seeing-eye
dog, from a brain tumor. She who guided
a blind master lost - sacrificed? - her own sight
at eight-years old and was put to death.

Her owner had died two years before,
known as Grandma Charlotte to my eight year old
who will keep alive this epithet for his mother's
mother he knew only from several visits

though memory of her will outlive quite a few
gilded monuments he'll see wrecked in his lifetime
from war, storm, fire or *coup d'etat*.
For there's more to this fusion of dog and woman

sprung from no mere function, but something
that happened, bound for fable. One sultry day
when every living thing must find shade
from the Floridian sun that eats all,

Charlotte broke her obedience code
and natural gentleness with a frenzied bark.
The old woman confined to her home
in her perpetual darkness thought

the dog hurt, but Charlotte kept dashing
back and forth, back and forth the way
a dog will stymie a cat. When she knelt
next to the dog who would not let her step

one inch more, she heard the problem:
the unmistakable hiss of a dwarf rattler.
Blind woman, courageous dog, the serpent
could take you both down. What to do?

She groped backwards to the closet
and grabbed the next best thing to a bullsnake,
a vacuum cleaner. The dog helped her guide
the hose to where the pit viper lay.

"When it went down the old Hoover hatch,
it made this flappy whoosh of a sound,"
she'd say with a laugh, petting her black beauty
who would flash her noble silhouette

against the harrowing light in Kissimmee.
And then as the next day wandered in,
think of the garbage man's surprise,
and how the dog stood at attention.

But that's how things happen:
from yesteryear's trash, a legend spreads.
And may the tale of Lillian and Charlotte
prompt wonder and fear decades hence.

Anthony Di Mateo

251

JUST A MOMENT

Flying ducks adorn
the living room wall
doilies augment
paisley scrolls
an ensemble of
porcelain dolls

Weary withered hands tremble
gripping the wooden cane
while hips sway
and dislocate
with every step

Quivering lips wrinkled
pouting at dismay

Ulcerated, bandaged
varicose legs amble
down plastic-lined hallways
to a door bell you twist
like a wind-up-toy

Mangy lap dog under arm
crochet rug in tow

Arthritic fingers
grapple with locks
latches and security chains
to open the door four inches...
and hear somebody say...

(in a presumptuous voice)

"Hi! ... my name is Mathew, and this is my friend, Mark...
Would you mind giving us a moment of your time?"

Mick Jones

IN THE GARDEN OF THE SENIOR RESIDENCE

Jean tells how she'd go to pubs and meet
American soldiers—she'd sing the latest songs—
White Cliffs of Dover, Berkeley Square—
teenager in London in the war years, time
of privation, of jokes in the bomb shelter.
She tells us in the fading light,
surrounded by wings of the building.

Every night, after feeding all her younger
brothers and sisters (mother dead, her father
an alcoholic), out she'd go—it was a wonderful time—
"Sing us another one, Jeannie!"—
as well as a terrible time—"The boy you danced with
could be dead the next week," she says.

We hear a siren beyond the garden wall—
a resident being rushed to the hospital.
An American married Jean, brought her
to Massachusetts; when he beat her, she had
to leave him. A nanny in Boston, raising
other women's children—when the husband died,
her sons began to visit her.

Tears in her eyes as we speak—
the new director of the residents' choir
won't let Jean sing solos, so she's quit the choir.
"My heart isn't in it anymore. They all like
my songs—I know the words of all the old songs—
but she doesn't want me to sing them."

Sing for us, I ask, sing White Cliffs of Dover.
"Here?" she asks. "Here and now?" Please, I say,
and she sings—her light, clear soprano reminding us
of bright nights when life was waiting
for everyone young to bite huge chunks
and down them with beer before the sirens wailed.

Lewis Gardener

253

AUNTY PAT

The weather weighted down
On all of us:
They
In their Corporate suits and
December tans.

Her cremation had lasted
Just fifteen minutes
Her
Allocation.

The vicar with his
Hollow voice
And electronic echo

Somewhere
Buried beneath his
Pulpit
That mucky
Mag'
One eye on the clock
False tight lips.

Only half her family here
Some 'family dispute'
Only ten people
Present her throng?

Sixty odd
Years ago
She worked those
Twelve hour
Night-shifts
Making ammunition for the war
Effort.

Fifty years ago she
Laboured in
Childbirth

Pushing new life
Into an
Uncertain world.

I had visited her
In the home
She was already cold
The radio still
Switched on.
She of the
Wireless generation.

As I walked away from the
'Crowd'
I realised they
Didn't know me

And they
Didn't know her.

Shown us another world in
Misty drawings
Across cracked window panes.

Two hours before you died
Aged eighty two – much reduced -
Lying there so very small -
I whispered to you:
"The Owl and the Pussy Cat went-
To Sea in a beautiful....."

And a single tear – a
Single tear - tracked down your
Cheek. A last tear
That I kissed away.

Roger Cornish

THE BAD QUEEN

She has skin like ash,
the shade of aspirin
and just as bitter when taken without water.
As I kneel to kiss her hand,
she says,
"That's right. That's how you treat your mother."

Len Kuntz

SAWDUST

Emotional outbursts,
uncontrollable tomahawks,
flying words cutting down egos
like Paul Bunyan swinging an ax,
making a house into sawdust.

I chop others daily,
angry house built on a hateful foundation
for a biologically connected coward
that left me with a female pile of sawdust.

She grew, cut down by constant punishment,
father calls her retard that stutters for kindness,
on bad days, he leaves scabs and bruises to remind her,
the oldest female is responsible for sibling's mistakes.
She comes to America to turn into an assimilated house,
girl gets scorned by a horny coward,
too young to know her emotional outbursts chopping at child,
cementing baggage in psyche,
growing in a subsidized government dwelling,
sawdust family surrounded by too many piles of sawdust,
other grains judge because they're from solid lumber,
and we're from particle board.
Our relationship is a battlefield,
two piles of sawdust
displacing anger like
a heart broken single mother
filled with dual role stress saying,
"Why are you making a mess?
You're so stupid and stubborn just like your father,
you don't even know how to love your mother."

But I do,
it's just sawdust is always dirty, Mommy.
Mouth never answers,
I become an angry house
with walls so high cowardly terrorists
can't fly over and hit my tower.
I protect ego, id, and super ego,

with wit that makes Paul Bunyan sweat to keep up,
while training for outside battles,
barracks are bone to bone contact sports,
until a punch injures eye introducing me to
an Old English man weighing 40 ounces,
man pushes me down flight of stairs,
 surviving to EKG beats.
Judge hands me, a public drunk minor getting anger therapy,
sessions with junior psychiatrists,
protective walls dissolve spilling tears from mental moats
formed while encountering too many piles of sawdust,
saying, "You're writing sucks.
God thinks you're evil.
Don't write; you're already Mexican, get a job.
Go ahead; move out, you'll just come back.
You're too ugly and poor to date.
Go back to your country, you stupid, pinto bean dick, beaner."

Angry house gives up its protection.
It quivers, because letting protective walls dissolve
makes house melt into wet sawdust,
some particles sprout crows crying through human eyes as they fly
watching tears write mud poetry on dirt filled gutters.

I stare at my mother,
sawdust family united by cancer.
I tell her about my dream,
building us into a mansion family.
She smiles; my eyelids become wood dams.
She tells me, "It's okay if all you are is sawdust,
I will always love you."
Tears weigh down lips,
I muster a mutter,
"You must make it,
because a bitter, angry, young mother
can become a sweet grandmother squeezing the cheeks
of her grandkids."

E.R. Sanchez

THE ASSIGNMENT

In the third grade
I was given an assignment
to write a Mother's Day card.

For a moment,
I forgot my classmates
and wrote from my heart.

In that card, I said,
"Thank you"

"Thank you for tucking me in,
thank you for reading to me,
thank you for not being mad when I told you
that I was swearing and picking my nose."

I wrote it quickly,
and in a scribble.

My teacher mailed it off
and I ran home each day in an effort
to intercept it because I was
embarrassed by the honesty.

But I was too late.

I sulked away from the mailbox
to find my mother reading the card.
And while I was redden by humility,

My mother said,
"Thank You."

Taylor Macintosh

WALKIN' MY BABY BACK HOME- LEE

Prelude provided the faintest of echoes October 1973,
Fowler to East Lansing,
the front-page rustling of a Situationist declaration
sporting the stern Humpty Dumpty warning
that words mean exactly what one chooses.
An instant of clarity in grasping the undertow
implied in 'the life there is.'
No undertow, though, only a whisper.

December 1976
Henna goddess introduces me to my first
cross-dressing chorus line
up up up in a puff of smoke.
But if Stiv Bators and Johnny Rotten are destined
to inform my spit-laden reality,
what is Donna Summer doing here?
Maybe reminding me of the tongue-curling kiss,
the angel uttering sweetly sweetly drunk,
explaining the canticle of disco.
Gee it's great after being out late,
walkin' my baby back home.
'The question is,' said Alice,
'whether you can make words mean so many different things.'

Long before George Lakoff pulled me aside at the campfire
with his stores of women and fire and dangerous things,
I knew the angel was ascending on the third day.
One does not worship the darling, approximate or otherwise,
One does not weep for the discos and embraces that might have been.
One sits at the bare feet at Grand Valley State College
to touch the breath of the ascended master.
'The question is,' said Humpty Dumpty,
'which is to be master --
that's all.'

Loring Wirbel

ROCK N' ROLL GIRLS

Glittering like a tambourine.
Shining as the only stars in a jealous sky.
The girls of Summer coated in lip gloss and sweat,
possessed the keen scent of a musky garden.
Cigarettes, heels and half-tops flapping in the pre-storm breeze,
exhilarating our adolescent senses.
Ripe as the season's first strawberries.
Foxy, fresh and walking like trouble brewing.
Holding court in the front seat of a dilapidated car.
Tape deck blaring loud guitars.
For a night, for a lifetime, the rock 'n roll girls were ours.

Kevin M. Hibshman

KEY OF CRAZY
... in awe of Katy Perry

She is a lovely, dreamy pill
so unattached and unafraid
laughing with an immortal trill
a most mellifluous mermaid.
Floating on stage she's all the rage
blood red lips, opaline eyeshades
defying every rule and cage
with feral glares and lithe charades.
She percolates and undulates
she flows and sows epiphanies
she fabricates and animates
spewing soulful absurdities.

Occultly cool,
arcane daisy,
singing in the key of crazy.

Michael H. Hanson

FUCKING INSPIRING

You
Inspire
The fuck
Out of me

Don't know how you do it
Those things you do, but
It's inspiring something deep
Down inside of my being

I feel funny in this body I've known so long
But this is neither silly nor serious
It's better than best
And even then, I know not
Whatever it is

It is goose bumps
It is the lump inside my throat
It is what you do to me
It is just what you're doing

You inspire the fuck out of me
Believe me, love
It's true

And if it weren't so dark in here, maybe you'd see
Hidden beyond the rose water in my eyes
Lies a clue for only you to find

So what do you say
You keep on doing what you do
And soon, let me come
Join you

I die to inspire the fuck out of you
Like you inspire me to do so good

You inspire the fuck right into me
More than any mortal muse could

Let's cut the cord
Let's untie the noose
Let's remove all restraints
Let ourselves loose

Why not share in this fucking good fucking
inspiration?
We both know we want to

What do you say

Let's inspire the fuck
Out of each other

And then
Let's call it art

Jason Brain

ROCK STAR

He loves her
the way a 16 year old boy loves
the Les Paul Electric Guitar.
Gold plated hardware. Glossy cherry sunburst.
Hum-bucking wet dreams echo
hot light reverberations
of stadium crowds.

Day dreams and classroom scribbles.
Pee Chee folders caked with ballpoint ink.
-Her stylized name blotted on blue-lined pages
of his black marble composition book.

She comes through the stage door
in the Music Center alley
between sound check and concert,
he busts her dinner escape,
puny supermarket daffodils in his hand.

Dark glasses of entourage
push him aside like a turnstile.
When she swirls,
cotton lace and a draft of patchouli
stop his heart.

Her "hello"
is slightly accented,
like not from California,
not like any girl he knows.
He stammers.
She smiles.
Chauffer takes the flowers.

Showtime resonates
performance hall too small,
cannot contain her new jazz décor.
Frenzied crowd shrieks against layers
of Fender Rhodes keyboard
chromatic guitar and hips

that sway like palm branches
in a Polynesian breeze.
Stage lights bleach her undulating translucent gown.
Blonde guitar slung goddess.

Thirty-three years
since she first blew stardust
at this gawky teenage boy

constellations still flicker in his eyes.
Though some stars are faded,
the poet dares to whisper
"You turn me on."

Jerry Garcia

THE ALMOST TUNED GUITAR
for Kateydid

she is becoming

she is
but she is also becoming

she fairly shimmers with all the what will
she randoms and exponentials

the elements vie for her touch
wishing to dust her smile

it is not the stars
but the shadows of stars
that timid at her laughter

it is not the wind
but the reverberations of wind
that clumsy in embarrassment
when she tales and whimsies

she is becoming
who she is
she is learning to own even the echoes of her footsteps

her song is rising
her choreography is swelling
she is becoming

she is
not the beginning but the melody
she is
not the chronology but the wash of color
in search of its own frame
she is
the drama at intermission
she is
the hillside of wonder
she is
the almost tuned guitar

she is
the really interesting parts
of the all night diner

she is
the silent pause
just before the laughter
she is
the post-punk screensaver
of joyful misanthropy
she is
the stolen dessert

clear-headed thoughts may find her
but they will not tame her reluctance to sway
no, she is her own loudspeaker system

she quiets and reminders

she is

she windows and possibles

she is

she is

she is becoming

David McIntire

ANIMAL PLANET

"Please leave me alone," I said in my shaky, high-pitched eleven-year old voice. It was just after school and all my classmates had dropped everything to look at us.

Kat just laughed. "Why should I? You gonna wet your little pants?" she mocked.

Yes, Kat was a girl. But she was two years older, six inches taller and she was on the girls' junior varsity wrestling team. I was a skinny bookworm who had just discovered his passion for poetry. Earlier that day I had slipped a poem into Victoria Lindseed's locker, seemingly unnoticed.

Somehow Kat found out. "She doesn't want a sniveling little creep like you sending her love poems."

I looked around, embarrassed. She took the opportunity and punched me in the chest. Pain crackled through my ribs, into my lungs. I doubled over. When I regained my breath, I pleaded with her not to hit me again. There are two types of people in the world: those whose souls cry with empathy at the knowledge of other people's suffering, and those who are enticed by it. She grabbed me by my hair and with a snarling grin, she hit me in the face several times, rapidly. I felt several of my teeth shifting around in my gums. Blood dripped from my nose. My left eye immediately began swelling. The school children went crazy like the monkeys on Animal Planet that are witnessing brutal beatings the way these kids were.

I was on the ground by the time the fight, if you could call it that, was broken up. The only thing worse than the public humiliation I endured was when I started crying in the principal's office.

Both Kat and her dad looked like they wanted to beat me further. My parents shifted in their chairs, embarrassed.

They didn't talk to me the whole way home, nor did they object when I told them I wasn't hungry and wouldn't be joining them for dinner. I was just as embarrassed so I took a painful shower and went straight to bed.

That night I had a dream about Kat. Our naked adolescent bodies pressed against each other.

The dream was so real I could feel the warmth of her tan skin, the fullness of her rump under the palms of my hands. I could hear her breath falling on the curve of my ear and smell the hazy summer air in her bobbed hair. From then on I sought her out and let her embarrass me in front of the entire school. I didn't care as long as I could be close to her. Besides, I toughened up and we eventually became friends, though she found other ways to hurt me.

To this day I torture myself with all the wrong women and still I never wonder why. I already know that all I've ever wanted was to feel her silky hair against the soft, bare bank of skin between my shoulder and my cheek.

Jason Maul

AMY

Amy grew up in a bucolic 1960s suburb of Madison, Wisconsin, the oldest of two daughters of a pair of graduate students. She had blonde hair that draped over both shoulders when she wasn't running, parted in the middle, like the actress Peggy Lipton in the original television series The Mod Squad.

She was generous and kind, and soft spoken, though when capturing a boy for her "team," her laugh grew loud as she ran, pure joy and a slight ferocity on her face, her hair bouncing like a horse's tail.

She'd have her jump rope over my shoulders and around my waist and be pulling me toward the capture base in what always seemed like seconds, that huge, wide, toothy smile of satisfaction on her lips, panting from her exertion running after me, or around me, her attempts at catching her breath not disrupting her joy at having captured her nemesis.

The last day of school one summer, when she captured me as usual during recess, she told me "I'm going to have pizza tonight! At a restaurant! My mother's taking me!"

"Wow. You're lucky."

"Want me to bring you a slice?"

"Are you kidding? I LOVE cold pizza!"

The next day, she appeared at the bottom of the ski jump hill across the street from our school's playground, hair in her face, her head down, walking slowly up to where I was.

"Here," she said, carefully unwrapping the paper napkin around a slice of cold pepperoni pizza from her dinner the night before, as if it were a fragile art object. "I saved you this."
"Wow! Thanks! I didn't think you really would!"

"I said I would, didn't I?"

"I have to tell you something," I said, my mouth full.

"What?" she looked up, as if for the first time, her hair parting over her cheeks like a curtain.

"We're going to India in about a month. For two years. My parents just told me."

She smiled, but tears were in her eyes.

"We're going to Greece! For a year! My mother just told me!"

It was the last time I saw my first love until one afternoon as I was returning from middle school on my ten-speed almost three years later. Her hair was crimped, now, and even longer than before, and she was taller and walking in a sort of lope. But I knew seeing her from behind she was the girl I'd wanted to see during my entire eighth grade return from overseas.

I'd bicycled around, hoping to run into her, and even played in a rock band with friends in the park across from where I recalled her telling me her family lived in the complex. I asked around for her at our middle school.

We talked about being teenagers, and her boyfriend, and how she was having trouble with her mother because of him. We both cried, quietly, holding each other like children. It was the last time I saw her.

Terin Tashi Miller

MY LONDON GIRL

Like an infant crop
We grew from a start,
Clipped by a staple
In an impenetrable grip.

We held a flash
Linked to our marrows,
A taste of a first fruit
As struck by lightning;
Glaring rays down our glisten,
A flame unquenchable
Burning in columns.

In a bid to unwrap,
We stayed divided
In two separate worlds;
Chained by distance
Yet undefeated.

I extended my ropes
To you in your end,
Holding onto my part
As you clung to yours;
Reaching your end
Daily from Nigeria
As you held your grip
From far off London.

In your portraits daily
I found perfection,
Watching your wonders
My celebrity afar,
Chatting like always
Our jokes in thrills,
Hearing our voice
From up our worlds.

Someday in a runway
A plane shall arrive

And we'll reach for another
Like never apart,
Chilling in gazes
As safe as our grip;
Our firm inseparable hold
Synonymous to our heartbeat.

Dowell Oba

THE PROBLEM WITH HUMAN-AS-MUSE, PART 2.5
(In which the key's hiding place is conspicuously absent)

Your letters have gone into a drawer —
the one full of things I never look at, but could not bear to lose.
I have put your memory there also.
The hurt of your absence demands forgetting.
The drawer locks with the careful turn of a key,
protection against thieves and my own sentimentality.

You spoke of collectible stamps,
but they hold too much meaning now.
DC Heroes are San Diego;
The Muppets are love and unspoken commitment;
Marian Anderson is the story they forgot to teach in history class;
and Star Wars is a catalog of the poems I will write.
Yoda for wisdom. R2 for humor. Vader for regret.

Ben Trigg

DUSTY SPRINGFIELD

No preacher man's son
could feel up a lyric
the way Dusty Springfield
fingered the crotch
of my parochial school corduroy
as I rolled on living room shag
watching Shindig.

Her bleached-blonde beehive
Her mascara stare
Her fingers teasing the microphone
changed this altar boy's adolescence
forever.

Her look of love
standardized lusty yearnings
for any blonde chanteuse
whose breathy notes
dared us to cross into
the backseat on prom night.

When she sang,
I Only Want to be with You
her words draped over
puppy love awaking
like a vaudeville stripper
offering only peeks.
She could not be touched
through the sexy bodice
of her passionate voice.

No windmills could ever
clear the epidermis slicing din
that spiraled her self destruction
as she sought uber perfection
in flawless notes
assailed by the critics only Dusty
would hear.

Jerry Garcia

NO ONE SPEAKS
for Janis

long husky beads of
white ass southern sweat
is rung from the singer's soul.
play silly, funny, the stage aflame,
the taste of dry rain
on her powerfully trembling lips…
ripped in hotter blue california. red eyes,
soft and lonely, shimmer like billboards;
early afternoon glows in paved mirage.
so easily she falls in love,
never lose faith they claim.
critics for friends in the clutch
it is true that we all miss much.
in this terminal oasis
the belch of eye watering smog
is clearly the landmark
of discernible blues…
at which we all have much practice.

Joey Alkes

THE WOMAN I NEVER KNEW

She lived in a dead world, but I don't think she wanted to die and looking at her you would never know that she did expire. But I think the question plainly states – did she ever exist ? The night is windy and through it the clouds show themselves to be thin, vibrant , one-sided beings, quite visible but no presence and I wonder if this woman became a cloud in that man's life. An object which is solid can be dismantled, changed or eroded away by millions of hammer-chips. A cloud cannot, yet I could not find any foundation within a cloud. Disaster can always get through I found out. I guess that is how she survived – when tempests arrived she drifted past. Sadly, vapors could not hold the beloved paintbrush nor possess the digits to render sweet music, and I believe it rained a great deal.

Jayson Pida

DOC HOLIDAY

Daughter driving
Wife in the back seat
Me shotgun

Exit 46 to coast
We're 12 cars back
Just witnessed a pile up
Horn honks behind us
Jacked up purple truck
Wife gives menopausal
What the fuck gesture

I blink

Daughter says
He's getting out
Tortoise tweaker
With a bad toupee
Light turns green
He retreats

Good fucking thing

I have to get a job Monday
My lawyer says I owe
Disability 33 G
I'm out of dope
Root canal infected
Wrote whacko all afternoon
In Sacramento, 103 degrees
Johnny fucking Ringo
About to rage on my ladies

I'm you're Huckleberry

M. Frias May

GINNY'S APRIL THE 17th
for my daughter

Sheets of rain have been
shaking off dust all day

and my 18-year-old daughter
is tired from stocking clothes

at the mall, and from
other drivers' sheer stupidity.

Life after high school
is like a horror film

with no villain. We never know
what to expect

without a man
in a hockey mask

brandishing a machete.
It wouldn't even matter

that we can't tell
if he's smiling, we'd simply

run for our lives,
which would be preferable

to spending all our time
worrying about

jeans we can't afford
and all the other things

that desire convinces us
are missing

from the rooms in which
most of what we own

lay scattered about
forgotten, like nearly everything

we once loved.

Robert Wynne

SUNDAY

she drove east
into the mountains

she wanted to fish
he wanted to read

they would share
something new

she never read
anymore

he never had
fished

she listened,
he watched

wind foam
the currents

Floyce Alexander

SESTINA FOR ZAHA

The architect with lost eyes wanders the world
building homes not her own. They don't look
back like homes, leftovers from a meal
for philosophers or a giant cockleshell
landed in the city where she's anchored,
tribute to the forgotten goddess of the sea.

Her children have that abandoned look
making seagulls cry, come to cop their meals.
Curves of steel and glass lure great shekels
for her inventions, her ships unanchored.
Her sad eyes owl-like on watch for the sea,
she perches in many countries of the world,

native of a soil where bombs may come with meals,
no roost for her birds, no shelter for her shells.
Her own country affords her no anchor.
She belongs to the goddess of the sea.
Lonely nights in her mind breed worlds;
by day, in chic cloak with a homeless look.

The peloric riot of her bag of shells
belies the fact she is an anchorite,
secret oblations to an invisible sea.
She has beheld the flashy eyes of the world
mistake, with ever restless, hungry look,
all souls, both rich and poor, for meals.

The architect with sad dreams casts an anchor
for those seeking refuge in an open sea,
her floating nests, signs from her world
inviting trespass, the way a child looks
bribed by toys promised after a meal,
plastic soldiers in sand and jewelry shells.

The work of the day gives way to the sea.
Erased from her sketchbooks drift lonely worlds
she struggles to recall in a vacant look.
All hope, she knows, is a meager meal,
but when a pleading voice twists from a shell,
time to ready sails and hoist the anchor.

With a lost look, she's back out in the sea
of the world, her faith in home and mystic shells,
offerings of anchorage and a meal.

Anthony Di Mateo

LATIN LOVE POEM

Hic sum; es ibi.

Si in medio occurremus,
demergam, quia

alas non habeo tui.

I am here; you are there.

If we touch in between,
I follow the fate of a
thousand seafaring wraiths:

I do not have your wings.

Luke Prater

INSIDE THE RAIN

Your cream, it has a richness sweet.
A daring, darling, delicious treat.
Your lips tap right into the night.
An access point to love and light.
Will you reach out and take my hand?
So we can push off from solid land.
To sail upon an ocean lane
And take our place inside the rain.

Brian Heffron

ARUBA

Here with you
tropical and quiet
our minds swelling
with the heat of
the sun

We relax oceanside
on lounge chairs
sipping happiness
through straws
the sun approves

basking and cherishing
a moment like this
we embrace
contentment –
this is paradise!

Joe Frey

LORELEI'S LOVE

"Oh, sailors, beware! Oh, sailors, take care!
Don't list(en) to a voice in the sea." - Gertrude Alger

In my heart I remember
How I loved you in an ember
All November & December
In my heart, a burning ember
Holding hope though I am somber

I dismember & re-member
The time we spent together
Was it October or September?
Memory fails - can't remember
Except for love kept in an ember
Sparked anew by lilting timbre
Of your sexy, siren song
Love kept in an ember
Sparked anew by lilting timbre
Of your sexy, siren song

Your wails I hear still
from my bed of rock & loam
Under the cliff of your perch
All year long
Decaying in a lurch

As I long to remember
How you love me in an ember
In your heart a burning ember
That you sing of still
In your solemn, siren song.

On the rocks my body broken
My beaten heart, a bloody token
Holding love in ember smokin'

Smoking for your siren song,
Your sultry, sexy siren song

As I long to remember
How you love me in an ember
In your heart a burning ember
That still, you sing of

 In your solemn, somber, sweet and sexy,
      Silent siren song.

Daniel Armstrong

CAPTAIN'S BEST WISHES

Dear Miss:

I give this note to Big Bob to give to you cause I know Big Bob's gonna be tending bar Tuesday nights. You ain't been here in weeks. For a year now you been real important to me and now you ain't here no more. Please come back. I'm ready for you Miss. To meet you, I mean.

The Second Hand Rose ain't the same place anymore. Your perfume's gone and now piss and farts is all you smell on Tuesday nights. Even Big Bob said so. I miss you very much.

Hello Miss. My name's Eddie, but friends call me the Captain. I ain't a real Captain or nothing. I mean I'm sorta a Captain. I'm the floor man on the Scrambler at Coney Island. I mean, I use to be. I'm the guy at the bar with the sailor hat on. To be honest with you Miss, I wear the hat all the time cause of my bald spot. It ain't that big, you know.

You look real pretty Miss. I mean there ain't been no lady in Rose's looking like you in years. Not by herself anyway. Not alone. I hope you ain't sad or nothing. I ain't sad. Being a little scared don't count, right Miss?

I know you don't like talkin' to people Miss. You don't like being bothered. Me too. Big Bob'll give you this. It's sorta like a letter of introduction, right Miss? You gotta show Miss. Please. I'm the Captain the guy in the sailor hat at the bar. Or you can call me Eddie.

I wanna see you smile, Miss. You don't drink that much. I mean you're never blitzed after your hour on Tuesday night. I respect that in a woman. You got all your teeth, so I know you ain't a tramp or nothing. You're a lady, Miss. A real lady. And you ain't fat at all.

Forgive me Miss, but your real important to me. You make me feel like a man again, know what I mean? Last year before you started showing up Tuesday nights I sorta let myself go. You know relaxed myself.

I don't know if you noticed Miss, but I been cleaning myself up a bit each Tuesday night. I seen you looking over at me, but I don't think you seen me. You gotta come back to Rose's, Miss. I'm starting not to like myself again.

Listen Miss. I don't want this note to make you nervous or something. You don't got to see me if you don't want. Not right away anyway. Things take time sometimes. But give me back my Tuesday nights, ok Miss?

Miss please, please come back. Tuesday night I left Rose's with pee stains on my pants. That don't happen when your here. I'm real careful, Miss.

Thank you for reading this note. I miss you, Miss. That's sorta funny ain't it, Miss? Missing you, Miss. I wanna make you laugh.

> BEST WISHES,
> The Captain (Eddie)

Mark Blickley

THE DISASTER SISTERS

Three exquisitely diverse ladies stood on the shore of the tiny island with their arms crossed as Randy approached from the ocean.

"Isn't this just lovely?" Randy thought as he waded up to the women.

"How did you get on this island?" The cinnamon colored woman asked.

"I doggy-paddled. No, bitch, I was in a fucking boat that's at the bottom of the fucking ocean right now."

"How did you survive after your ship crashed into the rocks?"

"What do you mean? My ship has been long gone. I've been drifting on a raft for three days and all of a sudden I heard Donna Summers floating on the wind. I started paddling in the direction of the voice. Was that you guys?"

"It was, honey. Did you like it?" The ebony woman batted her eyes at Randy.

"Sure, it was fabulous. Say, is that a pack of cigarettes over there? You really got a pack of smokes on this shit-sandwich?" Randy went over to the pile of what looked like trash, but as he rummaged he saw it was men's personal effects. He kept an eye out for the shady women until he found a match and took his first drag in seventy two hours.

"Oh God, that feels so good. Say, who are you ladies and what are you doing with a pile of dead men's belongings?"

"We're the sirens." You're the first man to step foot on this island and not fall at our feet." The cream-colored girl pouted.

Randy waved a hand. "Ha! You Neapolitan ladies are scrumptious with your chocolate, vanilla and strawberry appeal, but you are barking up the wrong tree. The last vagina I touched was the day I was born, and I have not looked back. Besides, the whole sitting-on-a-desert-island-waiting-to-destroy-men-thing is so passé."

"Are you judging us?" all three asked.

"Oh honey, no. I've wrecked many a man's life. I'm just saying you could do so much better for yourselves. Live in penthouses while men below destroy themselves for you. I tell you what, you get me off this island and we'll take New York together. I live in a dump right now, but with looks like yours we won't need money. I'll show you how to manipulate men, and you cut me in, deal?"

Randy and the sirens left the island that night. When they landed in New York, Randy kept his word. He and the sirens were squished in his basement apartment for only a couple weeks before Randy helped each woman land themselves a gullible fish. The sirens are actually kind of famous now. This writer is not at liberty to mention their names, but one had a reputable acting/singing career.

The second purposely leaked a sex tape of her with someone famous and landed her own reality show.

And the third made a moderate career of politics, despite the photographs of her holding a machine gun, wearing a skimpy bikini and a man-killing smile.

Jason Maul

VACUUMING NIRVANA

I used to cower in my room
every time my mother vacuumed,
turn up the volume on Supertramp

or Pink Floyd and wait out
that cacophony of suction.
Tiny bristles bore their way

into my brain, sound bleeding
through the closed door
until I was finally certain

Buddhism was not for me.
I never found peace
in daily chores, never focused

so clearly on one thing
I shut out everything else
to find temporary beauty

in repetition. I still don't.
But my wife has taught me
the wonder of headphones:

now I can easily guide
the whirring purple cylinder
across the unsuspecting floor

and pretend I'm back in that bedroom
or even on a plane, engines wild
on each wing, carrying me

somewhere I'm not responsible
for dog hair and dust, where
a Frank Sinatra ballad

can be clearly heard
over the small sounds of coins
breaking water's smooth surface.

Robert Wynne

LOVE & SLAUGHTER

Sheep are by a goat while
cattle are like swine, prodded, yet
cattle go by hammer while
swine are by the hind leg hung
then swung about to spigot.
Quicker, infinitely cleaner, is
the hacksaw of sweet Susan's laughter.

Donal Mahoney

NATURAL PRIORITIES

I know how you like to concentrate deeply
when examining produce, and when talking with me

You can't do both at the same time,
or you'll stand frozen and confused

next to a crate of seedless watermelon
wondering what it all means

It makes sense now
the time in bed you yelled out "Mango!"

I won't even tell you what you've shouted to me
in the produce section

Rick Lupert

WHILE YOU'RE WAITING

I know
I know
I'm not what you dreamed about
but you could have Love
while you're waiting
for perfection

Steven Sassmann

FAT BACK

I sat on the curb and sighed. Of course I'd been stood up. I knew that chick was too hot to keep a date with a poor skinny dork like me. As I stared at a crack in the street, wishing it would swallow me up, a 2012 Corvette convertible with chrome rims, dual exhaust and a juicy, fat back end stopped at the traffic light. I would've had half a chance with the hot chick if I owned a car like that.

It took me a moment to realize the girl in the driver's seat of the Corvette was staring back at me. What a pity, I thought as the two hundred and fifty pound woman smiled at me.

"What are you doing, handsome?" she asked.

I shrugged. "Nothing."

"A ride in a convertible on a beautiful day always cheers me up," she said. "Why don't you join me?"

I tried to think up an excuse before she said, "Come on, I'll let you drive."

I couldn't turn her down. And she was right: The sweet summer wind in my hair mixed with the Dub Step that thumped out of her sweet sound system did make me feel much better. We ended up at the park, where I rejected many of her advances. If only her face had been slightly attractive I would've let her give me a BJ, but it looked like two frogs got squashed while fucking in a waffle iron.

"It's not fair," she chortled, "I never get the ones I want."

"There are men out there that are into, well, big women."

"Yeah. But they only want me for my body."

I let silence highlight the awkwardness.

"I had breasts when I was five, if you can believe it."

I could. At twenty four, not only did she have triple D's, but her back boasted a sizable rack as well.

They were barely noticeable, but my father's friend noticed them. He got me alone in my room and said he wanted to play a game. All I had to do was take my shirt off. He pulled out his cock and fondled me until I was covered in his cum. Then he took me on a ride in his convertible and bought me some cheese cake.

"For a long time I thought it was wrong, him bribing me to keep my mouth shut. But what is the definition of right and wrong? God is a man, isn't he? He shoved us into this world of shit. Every now and then He throws us a bone, calls it a small miracle and expects us to bow at His feet."

And then her sobbing, heaving mass was upon me. It was such a strange sensation of relief that I now have my own odd confession to make: Every time I'm down in the dumps, I look for a fat chick to cry on my shoulder."

Jason Maul

HOTWIRED WOMEN WEAR BLACK JEANS

A hotwired automobile,
faster than ever.
The neighborhood has two dead eyes.
At night they wear black-patches.

A woman cannot have a hip
without the grindhouse details,
cannot live without one
and not receive
a cold wind whistling past.

Mother they chose me
for a nightmare.
Should I call the authority
or use it for a long road?

The hotwired vroom returning,
the mother killed
a golden insect
once.

It still returns through two black eyes
between the rows of lights.

Kushal Poddar

DEAR BAILEY

I decided not to send you a statement from my body shop, aside from sheer lethargy, the damage wasn't that bad to begin with. I couldn't pop my trunk at first, but that wasn't something a few minutes of hopping up and down on my bumper couldn't fix.

Honestly, the effort wouldn't have been worth the trouble. Let's be straight; I'm not the kind of guy that already has a body shop, so I woulda had to find one open past 5, bring the car in at a mutually agreeable time, shake hands with the mechanic, find just the right moment when he looks away and wipe my hand off, review the estimate, harass the mechanic about the estimate, and settle on the price.

On the drive home, I woulda had to feel bad about arguing labor cost to the mechanic in light of today's economy, I mean auto shops always look so run down. I woulda had to keep my car at the shop a night or three and rent another one, and you know how rental cars are; like wearing dirty white shoes a couple sizes too small that always vaguely smell of vomit and cigarettes.

I woulda had to empty out my wallet and find your business card, look at it, stare at it, maybe twirl it around in my fingers a few times, decide I'm too much of a chicken shit and text message you instead, after a exchanging texts realize you don't have a fax, and neither do I, why would I, arrange a meeting between us, and try not to ogle you like I did the day we met.

Remember a few weeks ago, when I stormed to your driver side, mad as hell? You probably thought I was going to get hit by a car, the way I jumped back when you opened the door, in that little black cocktail dress, adjusting it in an act of hip shifting that would've been criminal fifty years ago. I woulda had to look shifty as I worked up the courage to ask you out.

I woulda had to make dinner reservations, clean my car, shower. I woulda had to bite my tongue when you said "granite" trying for "granted" over salads, pretend to know how to dance after dinner, and go home frustrated without so much as a peck on the check. I woulda had to ask you out on a second date, answer your phone calls out with the guys, go on a third or fourth date, get shit-housed, stumble down to the corner liquor store hoping they have condoms, say sorry a dozen times and thank you. I woulda had to say no to moving-in with you. I woulda had to kill my imagination for the two months you disappeared to find yourself in Europe (or was it Southeast Asia, or was it Barstow), I woulda had to pick you up from the airport, conjure tears to christen our reunion, ignore your traveller's scent, save for money for a ring, make reservations, get my knee dirty, and deal with people applauding me publicly, which I usually take issue with.

I woulda had to plan a wedding, buy a house, start my 401k, furnish a nursery, pay tuition, go to baseball games, pick up our kid from lock-up one night, cry at their wedding, hug our grandchildren, and write my will.

Then one day, when we go to things that are early bird, when we save coupons from junk mail and send our kids newspaper clippings that they will inevitably throw away, when we watch the same programs every night at the same time, when we are on medicare, I will realize that I never loved you to begin with.

I'm sorry I feigned whiplash for sympathy.

Bailey, I've decided not to go to all the trouble. I won't be sending you an invoice. You'll be hearing from my insurance shortly.

Kris Huelgas

302

BREAKING AWAY

Don't break the rules, they told you. It is not
appropriate for you to take the spot
we've given you and use it to engage
in things that undermine our heritage.
Don't question things, don't cry, don't stir the pot

unless you're making casserole, or hot
meals for your man. Think twice before you trot
out your own ideas. Girls of your age
        don't break the rules.

This dying band assumed that they could blot
out such a force of nature with a shot
of god and apple pie. But all the rage
they vented only proved you're at the stage
you'll not survive if you, bound by their knot,
        don't break the rules.

Andrew Kreider

NATIONAL WOMEN'S MONTH

It's National Women's Month
All over America dinners are burning
Men are starving in the streets
Their eyes gone red with the madness of celibacy
This is Lysistrata taken to apocalyptic proportions
And it must end at once!

I will no longer accept warm beer!
I will no longer stare vacantly into a refrigerator
Made pathetic by its emptiness!

Damn you, woman!
With your tits and your hair curlers
We have made our concessions
We gave you the goddamned vote
And what did you give us?
George W. Bush.
Twice!

National Women's Month is a national crisis
Babies aren't being born
Our testicles have gone bluer than the most perfect azure sky
Prescriptions aren't getting hopelessly abused
And across these great American plains
There sits countless copies of Cosmopolitan, unread!
Women of the world:
We men beg of you
We implore you
With your short, short skirts and your furry little boots
Step back into the fold
Use your wisdom to see this month for what it really is: March.
The month of basketball and spring.
The month of lambs and lions and other fluffy things.

Come back to me woman
And bring me a beer while you're at it.

Then come next March
When again you are overtaken by indignant feminist rage
Think of the men

Think of what they would do without you
And of how a man, lacking a cold beer and a good woman,
Is not a man at all.

Ramshackle Tim

I GOT A JOB FOR YOU WOMAN

i got a job for u woman
a jive thang
nine to five thang
more dead than alive thang

a slave thang
nigga behave thang
a lawful thang
but a damned awful thang
a shit thang
work like a dog
and watch him sit thang
a whack thang
nigga get back thang

not like my
street thang
my sweet thang
my can't be beat thang
my places to go
and people to meet thang
my fat stash thang
my easy cash thang
my cool thang
my golden rule thang
my can't hold me back thang
my sharp as a tack thang
my slick thang
my don't hit a lick thang
my flip thang
my shoot from the hip thang
my soothe thang
my smooth thang
my move and groove thang
but now i've got a grind thang
a run like hell just to fall behind thang
a not my thang
a his thang
a clean the toilet sweep the floor thang
a work like hell just to be poor thang

a rotten thang
a just another nigga forgotten thang
a bow and bend thang
a see no end thang
a make me old thang
a lose my soul thang

and you got the nerve to say
i don't act like i really love you

hell....

i got a job for you woman....

Johnny Wright

THE HOUSEWIFE, THE ASTRONAUT & THE COWBOY

women in the company of women talk too much.
men in the company of women talk too little
what is there to talk about?
says in Talmud don't talk to your wife at night
what you did all day, she will never approve
romance for the girls business for the boys
she is a rock that will not move,
he wants to cut to the quick
she wants to talk first to get to know you,
she's artistic and smooth
he's just a prick!

so he talks to her, tells her what she wants to hear,
by trial and error a lot to assure and just enough fear
to make her tremble,
a whisper in her ear to make her feel more secure
she always says no when she means yes
all he wants is to undress her, but no
she really longs for him to ravage her
to rip off her clothes in her cave, yes yes no no go fast go slow
a stranger no less would do it just so
make her his slave, then play the violin

how can you fuck so many women without loving them
i once asked my brother
i loved them all, he replied
as only 'men in the company of men' talk truly

the housewife the astronaut and the cowboy,
all women have two men between their legs, one for each leg
a boy who dreams of her in heaven, the poet on a leaf
and buffalo bill to hunt to kill
and bring home the beef

E.L.Freifeld

THEIR OWN PLANET

The world was too large, full of vast points of distance, so Sal and Crystal went away for a weekend to their own planet, undiscovered and fairly close. It was small and when they lay down together, her head rested on his shoulder and their legs wrapped completely around the orb. At the end point their feet nestled on top of each other.

When they made love on it, Crystal said, she felt a earthquake.

"Shut up," Sal said. "Planet-quake! Don't talk about that other place. This is a tiny planet that I'd like to stay on it forever. It has everything we need."

"Water?"

"You may not see it, but I'm sure we're lying in it."

"Food?"

"We can eat if we want---there's a restaurant right around the bend. More importantly is that we can talk...feel good. There is so much to feel bad about on earth, I wish I didn't have to return there."

"We have to go back at some point."

"Do we?"

"Yes. That's the gravity of it."

"Can we dance first?"

They stood up and wobbled as if rising from an all-day barstool. They made bad-ass faces, and laughed until the weight of the affair pushed their planet back into the earth's atmosphere. There was a burst of fire, and their pieces fell mostly in the ocean, but some fell into houses on the Eastern seaboard and many of the larger chunks were found spread all over Oklahoma, Louisiana and Texas.

Timothy Gager

ADAM IN THE GARDEN

blinded by the gaseous beauty
of this mother planet
i descend into a layer of existence
thick as any anywhere;
and in the crossfire of her knowing eyes
i can barely locate the shooters
whose arrows laugh hysterically at me
through the graveyard mist of my passion.

i am adam in the garden,
between the gutter and the stars.
i have been warned not to bite the apple
but i could not help myself.

she is a world torn to shreds,
a canvas desecrated
by a madman's razor;
and ripped page by page
from every smile that suggests deceit...
from every testimony that buys revision,
from every fanaticism that fills our insatiable tanks,
and drives us to the edge.

so you are the intoxicant,
and i am defenseless, lost, alone
and scratching like a cat
at the floor legs of your skin.
looking for relief,
you are the salve to satisfy
the incoherence of my itch,
a wayward star
in an incontrovertibly
screwed universe.

Joey Alkes

MOM REMEMBERS LITTLE ABOUT ROSWELL

she is captured by her little girl desires
taken away by dreams of specialness
discovering a new world in the light
of a falling star that was her spaceship

she shows them where the light bent down
on the horizon of her little girl twilight sky
she shows them where it crashed into the ground
the smoldering wreckage drawing them closer
she is told to never speak of this vision aloud
she is told that she did not see anything at all
she is just a little girl who sees lights in the sky
as they move around her
most of the time alone

the lights talk to her like no one else does
the lights make her feel better than the dark
the dark only tells her loneliness like a little girl
should never know but many know it anyway

she flies away with the lights in her dreams
she is covered in the warmth of lights
that crash down from the sky at night
falling into velvet metal pieces
that she bends down to touch
gently at her feet
she swears to them
she will never tell anyone
a woman remembers herself
humbled by lights from the sky
crashing to the earth at her feet
being told to never speak of it

she holds her children close at night

she tells them not to fear the light
far away up in the sky as it moves
it is her secret friend of specialness
made into something else by change
something she kept quiet about
something she never forgot

the years that went by with a secret inside
she doesn't want to talk about them too much
but when she does her eyes light up bright
she lets a little secret out about specialness
it takes her away to the time of little girls
looking into the night sky for something
that might take them away from there
that might save them from a terrible
form of loneliness

she tells the secret
only a little
at a time now
little by little
she seems afraid that
if she told it all at once
she might lose that last
memory of light
crashing to the feet
of a little girl
giving her the gift
of specialness
giving her the curse
of a top secret
to keep forever
even after
the little girl
has been gone
for so long   A. Razor

WHEN WE WERE YOUNG

When we were young, you and I, and we inhabited indigo dreams and dragonfly kisses, the world appeared open, inviting, for the taking, and as I lay beside you, making snow angels in powdery ice, the sun whispering through hushed clouds, I detached from fluttery insincerities painted by those clowns who forsake the fantasies of the impressionable youth. I knew the Universe would provide, and I believed, as children will do. But that was long ago, and life drove her locomotive past cornflower truths, leaving me in this wreckage, with you staring through amber twilight, accusingly, across mangled train tracks. The distance has caused me to wonder if we had trusted each other, if we had loved more, cried less, made a pact to persevere, rather than submit to scarlet pretenses, would I now be standing where I am, and would you reach across these weathered webs and grasp my hand? And would I allow the showering of ginger promises to wash over hidden deceit? The truth is the chasm is too massive and my meager pleas of "I love you" echo back to me, reflecting off your translucent skin, and I can only watch and wonder. I watch and I wonder as you walk, as you push Mars into Jupiter, leaving me alone in cobalt silence.

Michael Wayne Holland

PASSAGE

we were splitting
in the sense that we'd
begun drunk together &
she was still drinking but
I now preferred horses
there was still intercourse-
sexual & also some
verbal-
but that privileged feeling
of being teamed
with another problem drinker
was gone

we were in Texas

the only place we'd live

& it was a solstice or
whenever it is
humans can witness

an egg standing on end

& we had an egg out on
a sidewalk of the apartment
complex we shared with
other drunks & gamblers

& she had her red
plastic cup of wine &
sipped & reported
the passage of time
on her wrist as my thumb
& finger prepared to let
the egg go

with 10 seconds left she
counted down playfully
& then

at our moment

I did my
share & the egg did
what eggs do
most any time of year
& for some reason I felt
relieved

we both might have
laughed out loud:
screwed again by

the world

then she tried

& failed

& we both kept trying
while that egg refused stillness
& time
eased toward standing
between us

Mark Wisniewski

THE TRANSFERENCE OF TODD & LUCY

It's a field trip. It's therapeutic. It's a couple of margaritas outside the office. Todd and Lucy sit on the patio, in a drizzle, under an umbrella. It's a test. There are goals.

Lucy wears a white sleeveless shirt unbuttoned to the fourth hole and a beige tank top underneath. Todd takes a cool sip, touches her bare arm up to her long blond hair which falls to her shoulder. Goals.

I'm trying to figure this out, Lucy says. It's kind of what I do. He asks her what she thinks will come of this. She says she certainly has developed feelings for him. He says he has as well, but he adds that he shouldn't have, this being a patient-therapist relationship.

She says, oh hogwash. The rain works in simpatico with the trees and the grass. The rain wants to live but it's a caretaker. She says she wants him to absorb her in a way that she reappears inside the plant, in one giant hydrating moment.

He tells her that he wants her to rain harder, torrentially nourish him and soak him until his hair is matted and his shirt sticks to his skin. They could, he says, be lovers but then when they are finished they would be dry.

We can work on that, Lucy says. But wait, I should tell you that I know why I do this and this is why we're here. It's about wanting and not wanting--- and then figuring it that all out. She kicks off her spiked heels and pushes her bare toes against his groin, her calve muscles tighten, flexing to a taunt round tight shape. I think I'm right, she says, feeling him become warm against her foot, the same way the sun feels, on a beach, when it breaks free from the clouds.

Timothy Gager

MONTHIVERSARY.

Somewhere dear, sheer summer freaks on without us. Such a time
machine I've climbed into, banyan syrup seeping from my
bat mask. Somewhere, pure eagles share their lunches
with each other. Massachusetts shares its lunch with New Hampshire
in summer. Brotherhood is easy above 70 degrees. When your bike
careens into September, you enter bother-hood. That's no good.
A blood cloud bursts with ice inside it. Right now I'm staring down
an ice goat. Not an animal but an actual iceman made of goat. It's
right there where Lowell and Summer streets converge.
I could sing to you about this but I'd rather sing about porch
bells gathering their pennies together. Somewhere, pointy horse
music steals into the reeds, O friend of August, you don't know what
it means to watch such music goad itself along for no reason.
What is the opposite of an ice queen? I'd call you it, sitting
in my ice truck. I'd call you "angel" if I hadn't already. I know!
I'll call you Snowy Urola – a moth the length of an oak leaf. It floats
from green to green; mum. Why say anything this engineless
morning? I'll sing. I'll share my five-months-ago lunch with you,
beautiful habit. I'll lean in and brush the salt off of your green lunch.
I'll rub these sandwiches together to make music we can climb into
like a July balloon. Oh man what savage music I could conjure
with this summer mood I've imagined.

Sean Cole

READER

With hands oily from a deli
  sandwich, I lunch
on your words.

Their music
  stokes and slakes
my hunger both.

My wet fingers
  stain the vellum
bed where your words

moan and coo.
  I reach a blind hand
for more wine

while turning
  to a new page,
with the other.

Daniel Armstrong

RICE - LISA

somebody should tell my sister
about occupational sterility and lowered sperm counts
somebody should tell my sister

about the carcinogens and dalkon shields
that hide murder in mother
somebody should tell my sister
that nurturing does not teach one to dance
that care is disease and not much fun
but some kids never listen
some kids insist on defending lives with shields of lamaze
some kids insist on sheer joy before breakfast
some kids insist on outmoded glories with no payment plans

lots of rice in my life this year
uncle bens in glad foldtops with red plastic twisties
tossed about stepped on quick become routine
like toys without eyes
like years without interest
like homes without love
but plenty tv
and jasmine rice bowls
i almost endorsed comet slowcook brown
but preparation is boring
and takes so much time
and usually turns soggy
i can't criticize
so i just give up and throw uncle bens

my sister is boycotting rice this year
somebody should tell her the thousands of ways
she made me and Cesar Chavez
immensely proud of her

Loring Wirbel

"An elegant woman is a woman who despises you and has no hair under her arms." — <u>Salvador Dalí</u>, <u>*The Secret Life of Salvador Dali*</u>

WOMEN WHO WALK LIKE MEN

They seem to be everywhere now,
women who walk like men.
With hair cropped in a paint brush,
bullets for eyes and knives for noses,
they walk long halls, hips so still
they can have no pelvis.
Then one day you meet one
and become her friend.
A week later you still wonder:
Are all the women who walk like men
wildflowers, really,
locked in a hothouse,
craving the sun?

Donal Mahoney

DIVING

At bedtime you shed your skin and dive
deep into dark blue sheets. You dream,
and everyone is acting strangely, eating your food,
telling you things you know they don't believe.

In the middle of it all, you finally recognize you have
always really loved shoes, hot women, and nice
haircuts, and you don't want to shave your armpits
anymore because you are not that kind of girl.

In the corner, a tiny baby is crying. You walk
over to cradle that fragile life, as the rainbow cord
stops pulsing. It is scary to stand on your own, you say,
and you realize you are comforting yourself.

Andrew Kreider

IF WE WERE IN CANADA, THIS WOULD BE LEGAL

For Jane and Amy

According to the wedding registry,
Amy is the groom.
These are the concessions one makes
in exchange for cookware, bedding, and bath towels.

The social progressives are having a wedding.
And we are calling this a wedding.
There has been pining and valentine roses,
promises whispered between shots at the pool table.

They have earned this,
their love wrapped in white lace and a "brides only" cake.
They defy convention the way hearts pump blood,
constant until death.

When we say 'till death do us part,
we mean a lifetime of the only way
we remember to live,
the lonely chased to a forgotten corner.

From - Kindness From a Dark God, Moon Tide Press
Ben Trigg

NOTES TO SELF ON VALENTINE'S DAY

I'm tired of your poetry's swirls and swoons
Misshapening her shapes in the shapes of your moons;
And I'm weary of your prose, how it shrinks and it grows,
Untruthing the truths that no man truly knows.
Just give her a look, an all-knowing glance,
A silence that silently silences stance;
And tell her in words that inhabit no space
Of the smiles that you smile of her smiling face.
You with your words so carefully weighed,
Orange as the orangest of orange marmalade,
Are lost in your ink, invariably wasted,
As they taste of a taste she has already tasted.
Why not just take her hand, like normal men do
And lie till the lies stain your face lying-blue?

Well, I'm tired of your constant complaining
As if you're reigned by black rain always raining;
And I'm weary of your woes, how they stream and they flow,
Unearthly unearthing the earth I bestow.
After all, one cannot be a man blindly wishing
Unless he's a fish of The Fisherman's fishing,
And one cannot be a poet of a name
If unruly he's ruled by the rules of the game.
Just give her a look? That's just a start.
But manhandling her hand will never handle her heart.
You with your tongue tied, pretzeled in knots,
Unspoiling you spoil all the spoils of my plots.
Take my advice: Embrace my orange prose;
Uncurling I'll curl till it uncurls her toes.

Frank Mundo

CRAZY LOVE

Ben could not stop looking at her. He wouldn't stare but watched her askance as she sat across from him in group therapy. She noticed and each time their eyes met, she smiled.

Ben thought her smile was beatific, angelic, numenal. He liked the way her eyes grew wide when she caught him looking. Her shoulder length hair had a sheen that magnified the room's light. He watched the round mounds of her breasts rise with each breath.

"Ben, what are you thinking?" The therapist asked. "You're smiling at something."

Ben pulled his eyes from Anna to look at the questioner. The therapist's glasses reflected the fluorescent lights so that they flashed horizontal rectangles of light that reminded Ben of the robot in "The Day the Earth Stood Still."

"Klaatu barada nikto," Ben replied in a Michael Rennie imitation.

"Excuse me?" The shocked therapist cocked his right ear forward.

"I was … I was just thinking that Anna looks beautiful today," Ben stammered.

Collectively, the group's heads turned to look at Anna.

Anna stroked her dingy, unkempt hair. Her swollen, nibbled lips smiled at the flowers she saw floating above their heads; her eyes widened as they morphed into rainbows that showered electric pennies.

"Anna… Anna…" The therapist roused her from her reverie.

Anna blinked the rainbows and pennies away and focused on the therapist who had become a gnome with super-sized spectacles. He was saying something that Anna couldn't hear but the words scrolled out on his tongue and she read them:

"Anna, did you hear Ben say you look beautiful today?" The words were embroidered in vibrant fuchsia lace that melted into vermillion tears dripping into a confused lake of letters on the checkerboard floor.

"I love you, Ben," Anna knitted the letters together to make her words.

Phillip Maguire

MY THERAPIST'S A LADY

It's all so simple now,
yet it took 30 years
to begin to understand.
It's as though someone
stole the primer I had
and gave me another
in my own language.
It's because you are
who you are
that I've begun
to become who I am.
That sounds too dramatic.
All you did, really, was scream
when you opened the bathroom door,
saw me wrapped in a towel,
standing at attention on a mat,
waiting in my thirtieth year
for the steam to clear
from the cabinet mirror,
waiting for someone
to shout, "*At ease.*"

Donal Mahoney

MOTHER OF ALL WARS

A sonic boom tears
through the still night.

A mother scrambles
to gather her child
from its dreams
broken
by approaching roar
of death above.

A distant mountain slope
flares up
sky rains fire
earth shudders
the window frames
a terrible beauty.

Closer, closer, closer
louder and louder
the deafening roar.

Terrified, trembling
she sits up in bed
clutching her child
its face buried
in her bosom
eyes tight shut
too terrified to pray.

The death craft
rumbles low
over her thatched roof
rattling vessels
long empty
and vanishes
among the stars
a disconcerting speck
in the eastern sky.

Relief
silence
but not peace.

Nair Pradeep

HOMESICK

Learning to treat radiation burns,
her mother was homesick for permanence.
Brenda didn't understand the word,
didn't know to want what she'd never had.

18 years and too many cities to remember.

Nights spent with nuclear warheads in plain view.

Belonging was the myth of consistency,
the knick-knack her family had picked up
in Japan, or Hawaii, or Michigan.

With adulthood came choice,
the determination to stay in one place,
the ability to know local expectations.

Things stay with her now:
a husband, a boss, a son discovering himself
who will learn he always needs his mother.

Now she allows culture to grow around her,
no longer needs to carry it,
as though she might forget.

From - Kindness From a Dark God, Moon Tide Press
Ben Trigg

DNA COCKTAIL

An ex and a why chromosome mix,
making a DNA cocktail.
Ernesto, scared heartless,
pushes Heriberta to abort,
she says, "No."

He leaves, a grizzly bear eating his own cub.
She is a village girl, black hair split down the middle,
light skin with a dash of Indian, lays in a lonely hospital ward
contemplating adoption,
stomach bulges like a water balloon.
I am inside with my back to the exit,
C-section needed, but I wise up, turn around, slide out,
premature, left to an incubator,
given 3 days to live.
She prays as her finger touches my chest,
promising to sacrifice her youth for my life.

Leaving see-through cradle,
I lay in a '78 Impala with a mother
unable to afford diapers.
Staring into my light browns,
she finds us alone in a storm of ridicule.
She tries to cover me
like a smothering umbrella from the judgments,
"She must be a ho having a son so young with no man."

She couldn't cover my eyes,
they see a family struggling to stay away from mornings
excusing ourselves to parking lot attendants,
abandoned to race against other rat families,
two legs short with a dead-beat shackled to our ankles,
keeping warm next to a stove,
home alone hiding from strangers,

not answering the door for no one,
growing up independent,
every day you looked at me as if you wanted me distant,
away from damaging party years,
going out and working left me wanting things you couldn't buy
even if you could purchase Disneyland,
a teen looking down at authority,
I hate that you're my mother!

Heriberta, translating adult Spanish through squeaky English,
makes me feel like an illegal immigrant welfare vacuum,
born American to a foreign example,
learning accents label tongues inferior,
I left your roof, seeking education to dry this wetback,
using university employees to colonize textbooks,
honor the name you gave me,
Erik the Red.

Every second away from your controlling attitude
made regret cover immature moments of disrespect
for you, an abandoned Aztec Princess,
forced to balance a home on her head,
so her left hand can lift a pancake,
right hand ready to punish,
timeouts can't discipline an attention starved son.
You were always royalty wearing workman musk
left to sweat for peanut shells by a stiff-dick coward,
fathers like him are more bitch than a punk,
more selfish than a lion leaving a cub to starve,
more foolish than a crow trying to fly out from the eye of a storm,
and even though child support never wet his wings,

Mom,
life wasn't your fault.

E.R. Sanchez

RIITTA

She had dark eyes
and this Latin name that seemed
incongruous in the teeth of winter
blanketing snow.

Oriental fabrics
clothed bare walls with magic,
in her small room by the harbor's
easterly flow.

A handloom crowded the corner,
thread hung limply in abeyance
to uncompleted studies
at the Athenaeum.

Half-answered letters
strewed the table,
easing the night of days,
her Nordic sense of isolation.

Russian filters mixed with incense
burning for some eastern atman
close to her migrating soul,
far from Finland.

David Mallinson

RITUAL

The traffic is worse than on a Friday night,
SUVs and other behemoths everywhere.
I want to fly across asphalt,
but I'm not important enough to alter the flow of traffic.

In a place where the cars have thinned, I enact my ritual:
sometimes with a wave, sometimes actual words,
I greet my friend.
A simple action to fan the embers of memory,
her details slipping away.

I wasn't important enough to keep her car on the road.

From - Kindness From a Dark God, Moon Tide Press
Ben Trigg

SOLITARY MAN

He was staring into a plastic cup with a puzzled look so near breakdown he might have been collecting tears. He spoke to himself as if he were the only person on earth who wouldn't recoil at his inexorable lament. I took a seat near this solitary man of huddled sadness, not because it was the only bench at Grand Central, but it had been an aging week of unexplained losses and unwanted gains, and I couldn't bear the exaggerated emptiness of the skeletal room, an emptiness that began before my sister could no longer breathe and thus no longer sigh or scream in the language she would ask for love, an emptiness of not knowing how to approach her muscular fire meant, I saw now, for a disembodied past. She had been, kindly said, a free spirit, a reminder of limits most of us so easily accept, flying cross country with her fourth husband in a tiny plane he made for her, ferrying medications over the border for her sick friends, creating traditions where none existed, naming children where none survived. The man on the bench, the kind she might have been drawn to, went up and down, down and around to the restroom, to the map on the wall to the big window where people left and arrived, arrived and waited, indifferent to his inner destinations. Now and then he glanced through old newspapers as if searching among the remains of the yesterday for words that he might use to be heard. As I left at the announcement of my train home I thought he said 'God's speed' and I wondered if that meant fast in the way we don't give enough at the time it matters, or slow like sadness is slow, interminable, long traveled.

Jack Cooper

BEGGAR WOMAN

Din of peak-hour traffic
cars, heavy vehicles
and bikes
tired, restless drivers
fagged-out commuters
and commotion
at the red signal.

Engines of growth
spew noise
and smoke.

I spend ten minutes
every humid day
waiting, sweating
at the traffic signal:
the beggar woman's workplace.

Her left arm
cradles her child
too poor, too young
to drive a car
or feel ashamed
of its mother's sagging
half-exposed breasts.

Her grimy hand
stretches out
and hits dead flesh
under my chin.

I ride home ashamed guilty
amid numb animals
in human form
in an unequal world
where the rich strut naked
the poor scamper
to hide their shame.

Nair Pradeep

COFFEE TIME, FULLER'S RESTAURANT
(Edmonton, Alberta)

June 29th, 1980, three o'clock A.M.
And I'm getting older by the minute.
Thinking about it makes me tired.
Outside traffic crawls slowly over
slippery pavement like inebriated turtles.
Inside, at the coffee counter, I flirt with a waitress –
fresh young fruit from Montreal.
She insists on calling me Vincent Price
and speaking French in Alberta.
I'm trying to read *Periods of the Moon,*
by Irving Layton, selecting the human
condition, repetition, and insomnia as
my main themes.
Next to me, a street gypsy drooping
over the counter beside me, pulling
scraps of dog-eared aged newsprint
from a doggie bag. She stares
squint-eyed at a picture of John F. Kennedy
for two hours, manages to laugh
an incredible 29 times,
sorry, 30 times, 31.
Counting makes me tired,
makes me take notice of this gypsy
and disapprove.

Michael Lee Johnson

THE VIEW FROM A SKYSCRAPER

I have never learned how to draw perfect circles.
The centers shake me off
like shrugged shoulders, sharp shudders,
a tongue-twister with all of my
past mistakes rearing hard, offering this:
a barbed fist
Gatling gun
guillotine blade.

I have never written the right words about you.
Even the letters get lost,
the kerning and tooling of certain fonts
bleeding and blurring,
the syntax of breath making meaning
out of ink the only way it knows how,
pungent and orderless.

I have never learned how to sleep a full night.
Some people find their power in naps,
others pull strength from Freudian jigsaws
while my dreams are less laundered
tattered fiction,
sprung screen doors
hinged in nothing but wind,
unhinged by the lingering scent of
your maladjusted ghost.

Len Kuntz

TRIANGLE IN WASHINGTON SQUARE

It was an ineffably beautiful day in New York City last Thursday. I'd come in from suburban New Jersey to conduct some research in a library devoted to Jewish culture and history, located in the East Village. I finished my work there by 2pm and walked a few blocks to Washington Square Park; I just read a book about the Triangle Shirtwaist Factory fire, and learned that the building which housed Triangle still stands, though it's been renamed and now contains classrooms and offices for NYU.

For those who don't know of it: the Triangle Shirtwaist Factory fire, March 25, 1911, was the greatest single workplace loss of life in a New York City...until September 11, 2001. Crammed into lofts filled with extremely flammable cloth and other materials, seamstresses, cutters and other workers toiled 12-15 hours a day six or seven days a week in the swiftly growing NYC garment industry. Conditions were bad, but they were worse elsewhere, and people were glad to have a job at Triangle.

No one knows how the fire started, but the minute-by-minute account makes it clear that after 60 to 90 seconds, anyone still in the building was doomed to death by smoke or by fire. Actually, some people chose a third option: jumping to certain (if not always immediate or merciful) death from the ninth and tenth story windows.

146 (mostly) women and men died; hundreds of people lined up for days to view the burnt and crushed corpses, to claim a sister or mother or child. In many cases the face was unidentifiable; only a lock of hair, a scrap of lace, a certain shoe brand, could give the victim a name. The tragedy sparked a near-revolt in the immigrant quarters of the city, leading to large-scale changes in workplace safety, treatment of immigrants, and the balance of political power in New York. The factory's owners were acquitted of wrongdoing.

It was eerie to stand beneath the building at the northwest corner of Greene Street and Washington Place – it had become so iconic in my mind. It was like standing next to the Titanic. I looked around me and tried to imagine what it was like that March day almost 100 years ago: bodies sprawled on the pavement; firemen shouting – knowing that their firehoses couldn't reach the fire on the ninth floor, running into the blazing building that others were running and jumping from; the slick streets covered with water, reflecting the blaze luridly in the setting sun; people on the ground shouting to those at the windows not to jump, that help was coming! It came too late.

Thursday must've been a visiting day for incoming or prospective NYU students, because the narrow streets were packed with smiling young people and their parents. Many had name tags stuck to their shirts. I stepped around them and past them to take pictures; they didn't seem to notice the dead, mangled women at their feet.

Dan Capriotti

MY MOTHER DREAMS MY CRUCIFIX

My mother dreams my crucifix;
arms outstretched, I shout to heaven…

Listening to her describe her dreams,
suddenly I'm thirteen again,

propped in her yard like the plastic owl
meant to scare away the birds that is now

hidden beneath a white blanket
of droppings, watching hummingbirds

flutter from feeder to feeder,
lapping the saccharine nectar

recast into pure energy with pinwheel wings.
"Matthew, get inside; that sidewalk's filthy!"

yells my mother.   An old bird alighting
on a budding branch of Society

Garlic, lunges for a lazy lizard
sunning on the railroad lumber

my step dad, Bob, laboriously laid
in their yard for a train that never came.

From my window, I watch the leader
hummingbird guard all four feeders,

his neck a swivel set to the wind's fickle rhythms.
Others approach, whom he chases away,

high on power and sugar water. She won't
let me put sugar in my coffee, yet she feeds

these things a quart a week, I think.
Doubling over like a bobbing bird,

she sighs, "It's my esophagus."

She yells all day and drinks the world's

most bitter coffee and wonders
why she's on fire inside, bridled

down, dolled up, set to work her youth
away with the tides, tied to a house

whose roof she was lucky to have
(held) over her head, a house

she kept so tidy you could eat right
off the toilet bowl,

cleanliness her only control
and writing my only release,

my hands raised nightly
not for nails, but flight.

Matthew Nadelson

SHE DOESN'T CARE

She doesn't care
about the scars
the screams
she doesn't know about the pills
about the tears

It doesn't matter
when the little fist comes
crushes your spine
pinches your cheeks

She doesn't care
about your tears
about your broken heart
It doesn't matter

All those days
all the nights
pounding the floor
bloody hands
crazy eyes
broken bones
it doesn't matter

She doesn't care
because all the pain
all those nails
were driven in
for someone else.

Hart D. Fisher

BOWL OF PETUNIAS

If you must leave me please
leave me for something special,
like a beautiful bowl of petunias-
for when the memories leak
and cracks appear
and old memories fade,
flowers rebuff bloom,
sidewalks fester weeds
and we both lie down
separately from each other
for the very last time.

Michael Lee Johnson

SANDY

I have seen your eyes roam
over me so many times,
I don't even bother to feel
them anymore.
One can speak with the eyes,
you know-
and you've been silent
for so long
it doesn't even hurt anymore
to see you staring at me
and not uttering a word.

Michael Lee Johnson

A SIMPLY TRUTH

She sleeps at my side
her breath caressing my face
our years of laughter -
mini disasters – the
little tragedies have

left the slightest
lines on her face
at the edges of her
eyes around her lips I

examine her calm face
her eyes move in
morning dreams her chest
rises and falls
rises and falls.

"You don't even know me"
she had said last night -
"you don't even know…me"

words that lacerate
and break me apart
the pit of my stomach
toxic with waves of anxiety

for all our time together
all our seasons

It's a simply truth.

Roger Cornish

A.S.K.M

absolute sweet k. marie
absolute sweet k. marie
absolute sweet k. marie

every time you take your leave from this "crazy"
you perform a game of
operation on me
what would milt bradley say

someday you're going to kill somebody
and it may be sooner than you think
and though they'll never bring
a case against you
it will be understood
between us two
no blame here, just credit
i heap upon you

and if we're not going to be
commited to one another
then i guess i'll just be
i'll thumb through the directory
for there's bound to be a vacancy
since there seems no residency
to be taken up with you
anywhere between these two extremes

absolute sweet k. marie
absolute sweet k. marie
absolute sweet k. marie

Mark Radseszewski

PULP POETRY

I hate you
I don't love you
I tolerate you (because)
I'm too lazy
and too afraid
to do what is right.

I am pathetic.

Bill Friday

PABLO NERUDA, HENRY MILLER, ME, MY LOVER & MY WIFE

The riptide is a red current of roil and cold and I wave
And she waves back. Heat has walled up and flattened
The breeze. Noon clocks in.

Neruda's knocking.
Henry has his hand under a waitress's skirt.
Neruda finishes up the last bottle of red and tells my wife
To touch the wrinkles he birthed looking into her eyes.
Henry bends the server over the table—is this pretty or what?

Pier fisherman reel in, cast out, follow the bounce of my lover
Approaching me along the water's edge. Straw hat, sunglasses,
Portuguese Jackie O.

Neruda understands a kiss after wine. How fragile fidelity is.
Henry sniffs—I love Tuscany soil.

My lover stands in my sun, gin on her breath
Tide salt drying on her ankles.

Swim out to the female circle, Neruda tells my wife in Galapagos.
Henry grinds—doesn't it feel like a cudgel?

My lover fades like a moon stain.
My wife throws my clothes out the window.
A light beams down.
Hat, badge, green uniformed Ranger.
Buddy, you can't do that here.

M. Frias May

349

I HAVE MOSTLY NIGHTMARES:

You curl against me
the coastline,
I wake to,
your calf
left a wrinkle
in my comforter;
a note

a funnel cloud,
destroyed everything,

left the foundation
and the coffee maker.

Timothy Gager

EVERY TIME

Every time I love a woman
I am soon asked to prove
An infinity of negatives
Which ain't as easy as it looks.

Every time I love a woman
I am asked to become the Magic Revisionist.
The past? It never happened!
Really… I swear…

And every time I love a woman
I must wear special goggles
Through which all others
Appear as cardboard cut-outs.
But they aren't. The bitches bleed
Even where they ain't been cut.

Oh, every time I love a woman
She fondles my flesh, seduces my soul
Takes me up on Cloud Nine,
Then whispers Icarus! and gives me a shove
To ensure that I fully understand
The gravity of the situation.

Every time I love a woman
I end up with my whole life
Packed into boxes
And no place to live.

Rob Dakin

IRONING BOARD

Carton boxes piled on top of each other
struggle to survive the mess of a room
where grips of clothes thrown to the opposite end
sandwich an almost out of place ironing board
neatly covered by a white towel.

Inside those boxes are all kinds of books
a man has read or intends to read-
philosophy, religion, literature and such.
Among the clothes left unattended
in the corner is the neglect of love,
matrimony not thought of for some time-
stained by the imprints of promiscuity.

But that board stands with a wife's hope,
though covered by the white towel
of a mistress's contumacy
and sweat,
pressed down with the weight of warring tenants.

It groans for the decrement of a wrinkled marriage
But, at the same time, reflects the love
of women who balance the miserable lives
of men too preoccupied with their own mistrust.

Nicholas Damion Alexander

MARRIED "LIFE" – POETRY

Married "Life".
Will we survive?
The shifting shadows of the valley of death—
     there are some lighter parts.
But everywhere the ground looks unsteady.
     Walking becomes a war;
        we were never ready.
Death seems a dramatic designation
     but I die in many things of ours;
not the least of which is the resignation
     that sinks down in the night hours.

I have no idea what I'm doing
     with my life...
I am torn in all directions
     on a map without directions,
placing possible projections
     on each passing piece of mind.
But I have no peace of mind,
     and my ego grabs the reins
     and halts the forward motion of my thoughts-on-
trains.
I have no way of knowing what the future brings,
     and I'm not prepared at all.
I had no idea being a husband
     would make me feel so lost sometimes.
This is strange terrain,
     with windy paths and fights so full of pain;
droughts would be blessings
     because then tears would not
     soak our souls like drops of rain.
But it's monsoon season
     for us both.

I don't know what I'm doing,
     especially when my metaphors suck,
     they don't bring the bucks,
and writing feels like an exorcism
     of bad ideas.
You tell me to put down the pen,

burrow familiarly into my side,
and whisper
"This is also poetry."

Evan Dunn

LOVE & HATE
for Kymberly Hollander

I didn't know – in truth, how could I have?

That you'd always hate me for loving you;
Damning me for the devotion I gave
In words that fade now in my solitude.
I offered everything to feed the fire
Of passion you kindled, then crushed to ash;
Desperate not to let it expire,
Like dying embers swept into the trash.
A day will come when I love you no more;
When I stop hiding from a harsh truth veiled
By the shadows in my mind, and restore
Sanity, accepting my prayers have failed.

"I love you" seems the strongest thing I say:
 It always pushes you farther away…

Bud Koenemund

MARCH

"E"; you know what "E "means. - Jaime Saenz

Well this doesn't look good does it. Squirreling
lotion and tissues into the bedroom with me. Really
my hands are cracked. And the Kleenex *should* be
bedside, it's where the sad happens. Who am I afraid
of scandalizing? Santa? I live like a spit
in a bay: surroundless.

Sure – she took the HER out of HERE, leaving E.
Jaime Saenz said "you know what 'E' means" but I
don't. Stick it on its side and shut the window.
Origami is everything to the singleton.

To build birds. That's what Capital "He" does. You won't be
solo with enough paper, this form of life needs property.
Prop. To prop up. To stick a wood sword under a beached
boat, let a crab crawl under. Oh Christ, fold me. I'm banging
around this house like a bee in a bell. Ringing zilch.

Sean Cole

SKÅL I SAY

"I put my mouth on your heart." —Rolf Jacobsen

Having held you
makes me thankful
for oblivion
our thinning yesterdays
our disanimated vows
passing through me
dream and bone
grief and grievance
like cosmic rays
The way you fell all over
my only friend in Bergen
whom you knew I loved
Crashing the party in Oslo
with your new therapist
who had already decided
I lived a lie

Still, intractable moments of beauty
survive our past imperfect
working their way to the surface
like nails in wall board
you playing Grieg
on his own clavier
me washing your back
shell in the midnight sun

We had paired up the two of us
made a go of it
geese for life we said
Your country was of us
then of no one

Your language, once ours
now the sound of one glass clinking
Skål I say
Cheers for the years
for the tears
Tomorrow is not for everyone

Jack Cooper

THE FAILED ROMANTIC

Wearing the mask
Of a scarred beauty
You led to deceive
As if it were duty

And when I examined you closely
I was put to the test
And charmed into believing
You were not like the rest

How foolish is passion
For no stranger to fate
I dared to approach
As the hour grew late

Dark as November
I fell with the leaves
Preparing for Autumn
Before the deep freeze

We spoke of love
And presented its proof
A new found faith
In your religion of truth

But as autumn died
Winter would bring
The reason we won't see
Summer or spring

You made love to another
And that hurt so much
And the flowers I sent you
Died with his touch
And yet I still wish
That I'd never left
When lovers part
For a lovers death

The inconclusive conclusion

Never ends in the heart
To continue together
I would still feel a part
Of a traitor to love
And I was betrayed
The love we had made
Now broken

The failed romantic
I have become
But the heart will restore
The feeling that's gone

Spencer Slater

THROUGH THE WALL

You hear me
Tell you
I love you
Through the wall;
The wall that

Separates us all
When romance sleeps
And habit plods
Like an old man
With no tales to tell.

You hear me
Tell you
I love you
Through the wall;
The wall that
Divides us all
When we find
Ourselves alone in
A room full of pictures
That smile and gloat.

You hear me
Tell you
I love you
Through the wall;
The wall that
Severs us all
When darkness shines
On our secrets
And whispers rest
From our embrace.

I tell you
I love you
Through the wall;
Although I wasn't
There.
I was in the next

Room.
But I meant
Every word
I didn't
Say.

Nicholas Vaughn

PREDICTIONS FROM THE WOMAN WHO RAISED ME

The wrong side of history showed up
this morning on my walk through the woods
where saplings, warped by the persistent sheen of summer sun,
had their spirits split open
broken like tinder or kindling
which took me back to youth
that scary place
staring at crooked linoleum tile
instead of eyes,
her hot breath like
jalapeños in my face
saying, "Boys don't cry."
saying, "Fairy tales are jelly lies."
saying, "You and your future don't stand a chance."

Len Kuntz

TOTAL BREAKDOWN IN COMMUNICATION
LEADING TO DIVORCE AND DEATH

watching the block piling
i notice not she who piles
just the wall going up
building bigger, miles and miles,
up to the sky
and off to the moon
higher and higher, no way in,
no window, no door, no cat-flap,
she builds her way,
never to love me again

Trevor Maynard

WRITE ANOTHER BOOK ABOUT IT

Two years ago to the day,
I took a long shot at salvation
Crazy purple and cyan hair
big leather boots and a strap on for the weak
I took a gamble
I put it all on the line

She had British lips
an imp's bite
deep hungry eyes
a cackle to curl dead toes

I waited for the payout
Hands out and shaking
I watched my nag pull up stacks
the dice bump up all wrong
and when the sun rose
I knew she had my number

Her temper flared
the little critter bit
and dumped me hard
1st thing in the morning
a premeditated drama
two weeks brewing
a carefully laid plot
but I had to laugh
it was all so scripted
all so written
no juice
all flash
all soap opera fury
seen it so many times
this time it didn't even hurt
she went for all the same wounds
all the old scars
but I couldn't feel much of anything

I was 31 for a day

and already I'd been given the greatest gift of all

I was numb
I didn't feel anything anymore
so I sat down
to write her this last poem
not another book
not another line

Just this last poem
because she just didn't deserve anymore.

Hart D. Fisher

SHE

She lives in a room next
to a room she lives
in a room next to a room she may
live in

An annexe she lives in an attic she lives in an
image she made she lives it for others
she lives? In a glasshouse an outhouse she lives in her mind

She lives in an idea of what she maybe
what she could be what he wants her to be
what others want her to be a mother a
daughter a lover some saint a lady
a whore a goddess - a shadow of
A fuck - a suck - a hole

She lives in a space inside a void
below a hole under some rubbish they
piled up she lives in a bonfire in a cardboard
fucking box under a bridge like a fucking
troll. She lives - She lives? She lives?

She exists in every street every neighbourhood
every avenue every boulevard every where
She goes on and she lives behind the mask
she wears for him for you for them
But not for me   She lives in me – in
my mind in my soul I know her I love her
and I'm fucking angry for her!

Roger Cornish

366

LOVE IS ANOTHER THING

Sitting at the table
spinning the creamer
running her fingers through sugar
the kids spilled at supper, Sue

suddenly says, "Don,
love is another thing."
Since love is another thing
I have to go rent a room,

leave behind eight years,
five kids, the echoes of me
raging at noon on the phone,
raging at night, the mist

of whose fallout ate her skin,
ate her bones, left her a kitten
crying high in an oak
let me free, let me free

Donal Mahoney

EVENING FLOW
for Addie and Eddie Vedder

I come into the room where it is dark
I put my tongue on your eyebrow

You tell me you've finished the book
You tell me we can see the movie now

I say *That's Good* and go into the bathroom
I am in the bathroom with the cat who is waiting for me

You have a wet eyebrow
You have a wet eyebrow in the dark

I do my business
I am sitting near the cat who endears himself to the doorstop

You notice when I open the door
You have bean bags on your eyes

I put my tongue on your other eyebrow
I am aware of the beanbags

You say they help you relax
You and the beanbags and the wet eyebrows

We will see the movie
We, the rhythm of the evening

Rick Lupert

MY DREAM WOMAN WAITS TWENTY MINUTES

has a white towel
wrapped around
her naked body
as she sits on a bedroom chair

wears a plastic bag
like a cafeteria worker
on her head to
incubate hair dye

uses chopsticks
to fish out
potato chips
from a zipper mouth

enters her new
job address
into the GPS
I charged in my car for her

turns on her laptop
to check our
bank accounts
changed passwords

her beautiful face
still has eyeliner
and her soft light skin
enjoys the fan

Don Kingfisher Campbell

AUTUMN'S DAUGHTER

she fancies herself a spring
even dresses as one
bright and vibrant
budding
but spring is supposed to be a beginning
and she only brings ends
the end of dreams
the end of summer's brilliant advance
the end of hope
her face
is as beautiful
as the harvest moon
her arms
possess the comfort
of a November fireplace
her voice
remains clutched
to my memory,
like the last of the October leaves,
trying to hold on
for one more season
a spring?...no she's definitely a fall
In every sense of the word
our last embrace
was shortened
by the chill
of forgotten
importance
and our final kiss
tasted of burnt orange
and decomposing
foliage
many times since
I have wished
this were just a
late April shower
but love doesn't turn
calendars
and storms
know no

season
even so…
I'm a man
I don't have to bleed
to be broken
I don't have to pass
to feel dead
all I have to do
is look into those
smoky eyes
to see that winter
is on
the
horizon…

Kevin Craig

TELOS

You have my recurrent sick headache.
I have your tea with honey and lemon.
You are facing toward Japan.
I have yard work to do right here.
Together we might make such a one
as caused the Others to pass judgment:
a Japanese gardener, rife with complaints,
and no place to look for meaning but within.
We make our way, now in lonely unison,
across an unyielding turf that could not care less.
We walk beneath a sluggish, low-slung sky
that is non-committal, perhaps harboring secrets.
But we have plans and goals, vocation, so we hurry,
our hands clutching blueprints and outlines for manuals.
We pass some who seem to approve of our haste.
Others merely turn aside to sneeze into their elbows.
You still have my headache and the sky remains silent.
Your tea has grown cold as our prized documents yellowed.
The light starts to fail and we must concede at long last
that one day the ground beneath us will open.
Upon its dank breath, it will utter one word, like a note.
Having tolled our name it will close, eternally, to chew.

Rob Dakin

REGINA

A sacred, spiritual day.
Our ritual.

Markets in the morning.
Lime. Orange. Lemon.
Citrus zing.
Licking, chewing, giggling.
Spitting seeds.

Noon at the zoo.
Camel. Salmon. Canary.
Birds sing.
Sliding, splashing, roaring.
Lions feed.

Sunset at Old Man's Hill.
Mint. Rose. Mahogany.
A longing.
Burning, boiling, evaporating.
Satisfied needs.

Warm silence until
Out of the blue,
"I've met another."

Sour skin.
Devoured flesh.
Petals wilt.

A new ritual breeds.
Stain-your-skin blueberries.
Bluebirds calling.
Lilac. Blue bell. Lavender.
Strolling through a field of forget-me-nots.

Mitchell Noel Kelly

RUSSIAN TEA

My two aunts circumference the garden
toting closed black parasols
in case the determined rain
comes impulsively.

Cups of green tea settle under saucers.
Afternoon shadows are the composition of pears.

My aunts discuss the day's adherence to boredom.
They might was well converse
about the proper way to select fabric blends.

I build wooden blocks into fortresses
near the picnic table and samovar,
waiting for the cucumber sandwiches.
If I wait any longer, I might languish in hunger.

The crockery has a pattern of blue pansies
to match our floral garden of irises and blue shadows.
A wicker trolley has some lemon-snap cookies.

I have been warned repeatedly
they might spoil my appetite.
Since when has a small boy lacked an appetite?
Waiting is not for a boy, either.
 Mother finally rings a service bell.

In the countryside we are isolated,
while outside things are about to collapse
like my wooden blocks.

My aunt's parasols might as well be
a soldier's severed arms.

Martin Willitts Jr.

WHY I LOVE MY WIFE, PART 6

Spring Saturday mornings,
she's outside digging
tiny graves for bright flowers

which won't last the summer,
watering until the earth is half full.
She spreads mulch, wheelbarrows

piles of decorative rocks,
fixes small plots of our yard
because garden gnomes with green cards

might one day take up residence there.
By afternoon, the flurry of activity
moves indoors, usually into

a book set in a faraway place
where all the landscaping
is already done. She folds herself

around those words
as if shielding them
from all we know, how

dirt and grass stain
everything they touch,
cleansing rain brings floods

and dust accumulates daily
from the constant erosion
of everything. She is vigilant

over all her kingdoms, keeping
everything exactly as it should be,
even piles of unwatched DVD's,

clothes hanging limply
from a still treadmill, boxes
stacked high in the garage

since we bought this house.
She is the reason
I know what matters.

Robert Wynne

MY WIFE

my love
my wife
eleven years and more

we keep the lawn trimmed
without concern
weeds grow in the flower garden
and we
still without concern

dishes pile in the sink
and coffee spills on the linoleum
but no concern

we love
in love
no concern

easy love
beautiful love
no concern

Jhon Baker

CATERPILLAR POEM

Addie discovers another caterpillar
walking up her arm.

We're not sure if they're coming from
the farmer's market produce

or if they've set up a civilization
in our house.

Three caterpillars
this week alone

each one found walking up
some part of Addie.

I can't blame them really.
If I were a caterpillar

or any living creature
That's exactly what I'd be doing

Rick Lupert

A FULL BLOOM

the flowers are yours.

wrapped bloom
naked,
plucked ripe,
full,
stripped.

to be virginal

and honeyed
in tactile, close
eyed
sensations
and warm, full
inhalations,
pressing close

between your breasts.

Jhon Baker

BEAUTIFUL LARKSPUR
for Sylvia Plath

the withering bouquet of a melancholy
mouth that bloomed as bright as a bluebell,
is herself encased for showcase

she beamed meaningful words;
poetry that could make the bud
of a rose unfold in the cold cloche of December.

Cocooned now in a quiet vase of
her own body – leaflessness.
Drained and dried, a stem, poised upright in her bed

Joe Frey

CHINA

Lady
I knew you

There was a gap
Between your teeth
You could match an army through

Hair
Disordered straw

Arms like laths
Sinews
Like strings

Your knees
Adorned with fists
Flamingo legs
Flying askew
Feet four sizes too large
For your body

Yet anyone
That saw you now
Sweep through the room
Elegant porcelain

Glamorous
In that dress
Covered with flowers

Would never know
That once you were
One bedraggled daisy
In a green field.

Thomas Kent

SURETY
for the wonderful 'walnut women' of Shenandoah County

Late July neo-Genesis:
yesterday, sun scorched, nut brown earth shards;
today, in profusion,
Lycoris squamigera –
Resurrection Lily.

Three months ago,
malachite strap leaves adorned this parchment plot;
with the solstice,
they became forgotten, dessicated tendrils
scattered by winds of dying spring.

Now, against all reason, a roseate nosegay –
borne aloft on pencil-thin petioles
(daintily defying the drying dust of Shenandoah midsummer).

Any of the town's walnut women –
birdlike, pruned nonagenarian relicts –
will divulge with twinkling obsidian eyes that these miracle
flowers
are more commonly called 'Naked Ladies',
recalling in the same breath
(with anachronistic maiden flush)
genteel archaic terms –
veranda; julep; gentleman caller.

If, with their airy florid terpsichore,
these seraphic heralds of autumn
can revivify parched earth and wizened crones,
Zion
still waits ...

Rich Follett

SPRUNG

Burying the burden:
burgeoning garden,
urgent growth -
bud, resurgent shoot.

    That leering, searing orb,
    hung from the heavens,
    demands flesh be freed
    from burlier thread.

Sprung, nubile and fecund –

    the female form fresh
    to a naked eye.

Luke Prater

GLITTERING EVER AFTERS

faith and me now it seems
one aims to reclaim these
while the other
struggles to hold on
benevolent armies advance
on two of these fronts
bearing gifts and forecasting
glittering forever and ever afters
i welcome both occupations
but they could not coexist peacefully
in my country
passion and logic, somehow deftly blended in
opening statements and closing arguments
filtering into both of these ears
i want to take on your last name
or we could trade two in for one
i'll make you better or
i'll take you the way that you are
it's a decade versus three months

Mark Radseszewski

I WILL PROBABLY MARRY STEFANI

I will probably marry Stefani
because she is the right girl for me,
because her father has a good business:
three daughters, no sons.
I know that business well:
it hates me, but it will
be kind to my progeny.

I will probably marry Stefani
because she has a respected profession,
because she is the right religion,
and we will not quarrel
over prophecy, or the naming of children.

I will probably marry Stefani
because she has a reasonable character,
fine hands, a nice face, an excellent physique,
because she has an inquiring mind
and is easy to live with.

I will probably marry Stefani
because she is a good women.
She loves me. And I
will learn to love her.

I will probably marry Stefani.

Scott Alixander Sonders

KALEIDOSCOPE AND HARPSICHORD

As I've told my wife too many times,
the meaning of any poem hides
in the marriage of cadence and sound.

Vowels on a carousel,
consonants on a calliope,
whistles and bells,
we need them all
tickling our ears.
Otherwise, the lines
are gristle and fat, no meat.

Is it any wonder, then,
my wife has a problem
with any poem I give her to read
for a second opinion, especially
when the poem has no message
and I'm simply trying to hear
what I'm saying and don't care
if I understand it.

The other night in bed
I gave her another poem to read
and afterward she said this poem
was no different than the others.
She had hoped I'd improve.

"After all," she said,
"you've been writing for years
but reading a poem like this is
like looking through a kaleidoscope
while listening to a harpsichord."

Point well taken,
point well said.

But then I asked her
what should a man do
if he has careened for years
through the caves of his mind

spelunking for the right
line for a poem

only to hear his wife say
after reading one of his poems
that it was like
"looking through a kaleidoscope
while listening to a harpsichord."
What should he do--quit?

"Not a chance,"
she said this morning,
enthroned at the kitchen table,
as regal as ever in her fluttery gown
and buttering her English muffin
with long, languorous strokes
Van Gogh would envy.

"He should write even more,
all day and all night, if need be.
After all," she said, "my line
about the kaleidoscope and harpsichord
still needs a poem of its own.
It's all meat, no gristle, no fat."

Donal Mahoney

LAST WORDS

Driving away From the cupcake store
which is now also a Mediterranean Grill

I say outloud
as if no-one else is in the car

I guess it's a lot more lucrative
than just selling cupcakes

and then feel a chest pain and realize
these might be the last words I ever say

I turn to Addie and ask her
What would you do if my last words were

I guess it's a lot more lucrative
than just selling cupcakes?

She says she would compile a chapbook of
my unpublished work, and that would be the title

I continue to drive, knowing
My legacy is in good hands

Rick Lupert

MEN IN THE COMPANY OF WOMEN

I have been captured, then held captive
by your lightning thoughts and oceans
of wisdom. I chose to listen, instead of
running my mouth to miss out on the
pearls and jewels of your intelligence.

I am only a man: mechanical, methodical,
unmoved, and muted at times. I swim in
your poetic lines to find my soul's purpose
all over again.

You chose to be more than my friend. More
than a late night lover. More than a smile
in my world of chaotic art and juggled
conversations.

You are my drum beat. My electric guitar.
My fast car parked without danger and doom.
And I am your instrumental that you
croon your most creative lines over.
The entire blend is hypnotic, melodic.

You helped me mend, ascend, bend,
be childlike and pretend, comprehend
love, transcend, and feel the delicateness
of the wind,

I am fortunate to be one of those
men in the company of women.

Christopher D. Sims

INDEX

For full bios and to view more work by all these talented
contributors please visit our website:
www.EdgarAllanPoet.com

www.ingramcontent.com/pod-product-compliance
Lightning Source LLC
Chambersburg PA
CBHW080951020726
47505CB00009B/2158